LAST ON
GOD'S LIST

CLARE HEATH-WHYTE
WITH JASON ARMSTRONG

LAST ON GOD'S LIST

A VIOLENT LIFE TRANSFORMED

10 Publishing
a division of 10ofthose.com

Copyright © 2023 by Clare Heath-Whyte

First published in Great Britain in 2023

The right of Clare Heath-Whyte to be identified as the Author of this Work has been asserted by her in accordance with the Copyright, Designs and Patents Act 1988.

British Library Cataloguing in Publication Data
A record for this book is available from the British Library

ISBN: 978-1-915705-81-5

Designed and typeset by Pete Barnsley (CreativeHoot.com)

Printed in Denmark by Nørhaven

10Publishing, a division of 10ofthose.com
Unit C, Tomlinson Road, Leyland, PR25 2DY, England

Email: info@10ofthose.com
Website: www.10ofthose.com

1 3 5 7 10 8 6 4 2

CONTENTS

NOTE FROM THE AUTHOR

I met Jason on his first Sunday in our church. My husband, David, had met him a few days earlier and just told me that Jason had a troubled past and wanted God's help. Little by little, as I got to know Jason, I learnt more about that past and his world of drugs, violence, abuse and crime.

To Jason, born and brought up on a rough council estate in South London, this world was normal. To me, a vicar's wife from a comfortable upbringing, it was not.

Jason wants to tell his story to people from his world – people who might think that God is not interested in them, or that their problems are too difficult to fix. As far as possible, I have let Jason tell his story in his own words.

This book is based on a series of interviews with Jason and his wife, Lorna, which were recorded and transcribed. Any words within quotation marks are their actual words.

If, like me, you do not come from Jason's world, you may find some of the descriptions shocking – especially where he relates his demonic experiences. But whatever your background I hope that after reading Jason's story you will see there is nobody that God is not interested in and no problem that is too difficult to fix.

INTRODUCTION

A few weeks before Easter, David was sitting in his study – in the rectory, next door to St Lawrence Church in Morden, South London. He had been in the job for only a few months and was drowning in admin. That Monday morning, he was desperately hoping for a few uninterrupted hours to work through his emails. Then the doorbell rang.

The rectory had a front door with full-length, clear glass. This was a bizarre choice. Whoever was inside could clearly see who was on the doorstep. Whoever was on the doorstep could clearly see who was in the house. There was nowhere to hide. And once David saw the figure ringing on the bell, he was certainly tempted to hide.

He had read stories of church ministers who had kindly (or naively) welcomed in strangers, then been attacked in their homes. Big, burly and vaguely menacing, the man on the doorstep fitted the stereotype of someone who might do exactly that. But David was a church minister, and welcoming strangers – however big and burly – was an unwritten part of the job description. He opened the door.

'Are you the vicar? I want to become a Christian.'

David hadn't expected that as an opener. He ushered the man into the sitting room.

'I need help,' the man said.

In just a few minutes, he opened up about his experiences with drugs, violence, prison and the occult. He had seen things he couldn't explain and he was scared. David considered recommending a mental health professional or drug rehab. But the man had asked for help, from his local vicar, and wanted to become a Christian. The other things might be helpful, but only the Lord Jesus can solve the root of all our problems.

Their conversation ended with David praying for the man, giving him a copy of Luke's Gospel and asking him to come back on Friday for another chat. And with that David showed him out, thinking he would never see him again.

But he came back. And back. And back. Seven years later, he is a new person. In fact, he – Jason – is David's church warden and right-hand man.

Looking back at the extraordinary ways God had worked in his life, Jason is overwhelmed by God's love. 'You would think I would be last on his list!'

Had David really known who he was dealing with, he probably wouldn't have opened the door.

CHAPTER 1

An old saying goes, 'Give me a child until he is seven years old, and I will show you the man.' Apparently modern neuroscience agrees. A child's experiences in the first seven years of life are foundational – for good or bad.

Given his background, Jason never really stood much of a chance. According to the psychologists, he was doomed from the start. Statistically, because of the violence, abuse and poverty he experienced as a small child, Jason would almost inevitably end up as a violent and abusive adult.

Robbery was a family business. Jason's dad served five years in Parkhurst Prison for armed robbery. His dad and uncle Trevor had robbed the Co-op depot. They had tied up the manager, taken him hostage, made him open the safe and stolen all the money.

As Jason puts it, 'They had guns and all that – obviously. As they were walking up the road with the money and the guns, the flying squad nicked them. Someone had grassed them up.'

But at the time Jason didn't know why his dad was never around. The one time Jason visited his dad in prison, he claimed he was there doing a decorating job. As a six-year-old, Jason believed him.

And although some of the 'jobs' ended up with a prison sentence, others were more successful. On one occasion his dad and uncle had robbed a well-known jeweller. The robbery was covered in the press and the loot had to be well hidden until the publicity died down. Years later they dug it up and hid it under a bed in the family home – in Carshalton, South London – where Jason found it.

'I was playing upstairs one day and, for whatever reason, looked under the bed. I found this big bundle of gold – necklaces, rings, watches.'

Despite hauls like this, there never seemed to be enough money around. Jason's dad spent most of the proceeds, and his time, in the pub. When he got back, he would beat up whoever happened to be in the house. Jason's mum was the punchbag of choice, but the kids suffered too. 'I just remember the home being such a violent place. It was awful. There was always shouting and arguing. The police were round all the time.'

Lee, the eldest, three years older than Jason, hated being in the house when his dad was in, and spent more and more time at his nan's. But the rest of the family – Jason; his older sister, Sally; his younger brother, Kevin; and their mum – continued living there. They got used to a cycle of domestic violence, ending up in women's refuges a couple of times every month. One time his dad found out where they were staying and tried to break in. The children were terrified. They learnt that there was nowhere they could really feel safe.

Jason took it on himself to try and protect his mum but, as a young boy, couldn't do much to help. 'When I was about eight years old, I went into my mum's room, and he was twisting her arm up her back. I just steamed into him. I punched him in the back. He turned round – and then I ran into my bedroom, jumped into bed, got the quilt, pulled it up over my head, and lay in the bed listening to see if he was there ... I thought, "He must be gone by now," so I pulled the blanket down – he was standing over me and he just went *blam* straight in the mouth. That was the kind of bloke he was at that time. I remember thinking to myself, "I'm going to kill him one day. How can you hit your kid like that?" I used to plot little plans in my head – "One day I'm gonna do him."'

Jason's dad was just repeating behaviour he had experienced when he was a boy. His childhood had been similarly abusive, and he had never known his father. His mother ran a brothel for the infamous Kray twins – probably the best-known British gangsters of the twentieth century. She rarely came home. When she did, she would turn up with different men who would beat up the children. Violence and crime was the only way of life they knew. 'My uncle was always robbing and thieving. My dad was an armed robber. His other brother was just a lunatic, stabbing and hurting people all the time. His sisters were pretty mad as well!' While Jason's mum's family was 'better', his grandad did have links with various members of the South London underworld due to his work as a boxing trainer.

Jason was immersed in a world where sickening violence was treated as a joke, and being left bleeding in a gutter was to be expected if you 'slagged off' the wrong person. He remembers a particular time when some people bashed up his dad. 'They was walking home from the pub and my dad was slagging off a local gangster, which was silly really – and two geezers were waiting with crow bars. As he walked past the alley, they just smashed him over the head with the crow bars. And when he was on the floor, they was just standing over him whacking his head with the crow bars. It only stopped because one of the neighbours came out and said to leave him alone or they would call the police. Otherwise they would probably have killed him. He ended up being in hospital for three weeks with eye patches.'

Not only was brutality to be expected, but it was also laughed about. 'Two of his friends thought it would be funny to go to the hospital, to pretend that they had come to finish him off. He's in bed with his eye patches and they had nicked doctors' coats – because he was under police guard and things as well – and got into the wing, and into the ward, and into the room. And they said, "We've come to finish you off." Dad jumped up with his walking stick, swinging it around. They was just in the corner laughing.'

CHAPTER 2

While Jason was on the receiving end of violence at home, at school he was the one hurting others. 'I remember a lot of fighting at school. I think the violence started because he [my dad] was violent to me. As a lad I didn't like feeling scared and that used to wind me up. In my head I thought, "I'm never going to bottle it from anyone. I'm just going to stick up for myself." If anyone ever tried to bully me or put it on me, I'd fight back.'

Even by the age of six Jason was getting into serious trouble at school. One play time he beat up twelve children because they were teasing him about his second-hand clothes. He was summoned into the head teacher's office, but rather than being punished, it was decided that he should see a child psychologist. Despite weekly sessions to talk about his problems and behaviour the fighting carried on. The efforts of his teachers, head teacher and child psychologist at infant school had achieved nothing. 'Because I was getting it at home, I wouldn't take it from anyone else. That was my thinking. I just wanted to be as hard as I could be so I could fight back.' At seven he moved from infant to junior school. He would still fight anyone, for pretty much any reason, but he was now stealing as well. 'I was still fighting and getting into trouble. Thieving and stuff like that as well – nicking cars and all sorts of things.'

According to that old saying, and modern psychologists, seven-year-old Jason's path was now set. He was a damaged little kid, who was already doing his best to damage others.

Jason was now at a new school where a less therapeutic approach was taken. Someone – Jason never found out who – decided that the only option was to put him into a home for disturbed boys. The home took lads up to the age of sixteen, and most were in their teens. Jason was only eight years old.

His time there did not start well. 'Your first day there they have a disco for you. I was really nervous – scared – because when I got there, there was all these older kids. They were all thirteen, fourteen, fifteen, and I was just coming up to nine. The first day at the disco, this kid comes up to me. He was fourteen. Quite a tall kid. He tried to bully me and things. I just punched him in the mouth. I got on top of him on his shoulders and I was just smashing his face with a custard bowl. Then all the staff come in. They jump you and beat you up, tie you down to the bed, and that's that for the night.'

The older boy was not just going to take being beaten up by a kid. 'The same kid I had a fight with before tried to stab me. It was about two months after we had the first fight. We got into an argument, and he went to the kitchen and got a big carving knife. He was chasing me round the house with this carving knife. I jumped out on this old metal fire exit and jumped over the fence, and then he was chasing me round this car. Luckily enough one of the staff members saw me and came and got the knife off him.'

The boys were expected to go home at weekends, unless they were 'naughty'. Unsurprisingly Jason rarely got to go home.

When he did, he had no friends to play with. He wasn't going to school locally, and the children he knew from before had learnt to steer clear of Jason and his temper. When he discovered one of the other boys from the home lived nearby, he thought it would be good to meet up. 'There was also another lad in there, Steve, who I thought was alright. He was fifteen. He lived in Mitcham, not far from me, so I went to meet up with him one Saturday. He let me in his house … and he started beating his mum up. I was just looking at it thinking, "I love my mum" – I was very protective over her – and, "Nah, this ain't right." I just got up and walked out – I couldn't believe what I was seeing.

'I went back to the home on the Monday, and he came up and said "Alright" to me. I just chinned him and weighed him in. I beat him up – I was hitting him from one end of the corridor to the other end. When he was on the floor, I bashed him up some more because I couldn't stand for that – it didn't sit right with me. So obviously I didn't have many friends there! I just kept fighting everyone.' Jason was angry, violent, and with little sense of right and wrong – but he always loved and protected his mum.

Some professionals did try to help. 'You go down in the morning and you have these psychologists' meetings. There was all the kids and the doctors in this sort of waiting room and we would sit and talk. They would air our problems. To be honest I was used to being bolshie and I didn't want to share much really. I was just really angry.'

Maybe the psychologists and counsellors genuinely wanted to help, but some of the other members of staff were brutal. 'When you did get in trouble, there were certain staff members who would just weigh you in and gob in your face – things like that – and hold you down.' There was also abuse going on in there – sexual and physical – from both the staff and the boys. It was a recipe for turning an angry, disturbed and violent child into an even more angry, disturbed and violent adult.

The sexual abuse was particularly hard to deal with. 'All these things that had happened had made me be not like a man. Letting someone abuse you or beat you up? You don't feel like a man inside. But you want to be a man, so you are fighting against that. It all comes out the wrong way – you will even attack people who is trying to help you because once the mist goes, the madness takes over. It was one of the things in my life that has made me very touchy. If anyone said anything out of line to me, or challenged me, I was just ready to go.'

Jason had fled when he was chased with that carving knife, but soon his attitude changed. 'Win or lose – I didn't care because I had no fear of living or dying. If someone pulled out a knife, I would run towards it rather than running away from it. I know how stupid that is, but that was me. There were some dark times in there.'

If some members of staff punished bad behaviour excessively, certain teachers just turned a blind eye. Even though Jason was the youngest pupil, no one seemed to care where he was or what he was up to. 'I used to bunk off all the time, because I just wasn't interested. I'd ask if I could go to the toilet, and I would just jump out the window, and be out and about in the grounds. I broke into the off licence down the road from there – we used to break in regular. We found a secret way in. We just took enough each time for what we wanted and never got caught for it. That went on for about six months.' The lesson Jason learnt from that particular school was that you could do whatever you wanted, whenever you wanted, and no one would care either way. Jason was in the home for just over a year. Just as he never knew why he had been sent there, he never knew why he was allowed to leave. He never asked anyone that question, nor told anyone about the abuse he had experienced. He didn't want to upset his mum.

CHAPTER 3

On Jason's return, life at home and school did not improve. He was now ten and in the third year of junior school. Added to the playground jibes about the family's shabby clothes were questions about where he had been for the past year, which he found hard to deal with. Home was the same violent place it had always been, with his father's drinking and domestic abuse. 'All the time home is just not a nice place to be. Whenever he was there, there was tension. It was just dismal. You didn't want to be round him because he was out drinking six nights a week. When he come home, there was always a row. The house would be smashed up, we would be clumped, my mum would be clumped – it was just ongoing. You get used to it in the end, but it does fill you with hate and animosity.'

And now Jason's younger brother, Kevin, was adding to the tension. 'My little brother was always a thieving little toe rag – you couldn't trust him. He nicked off me – though he was a bad robber. And Kevin couldn't really fight but he would try. He was a scumbag really. But my dad made him like it. He was a spoilt little brat which made him really horrible. And my dad brought him up in a way to hate us. It caused animosity between us and Kevin. When Kevin started becoming a problem when he was older – sort of ten years old – my dad pushed him away and didn't want to know him anymore. He blamed it all on my mum. That's why I think Kevin had a lot of problems.'

Jason's behaviour hadn't improved either. He was 'just fighting, fighting, fighting' all through school. 'I was known as someone who always wanted a fight.' However, two things happened that had the potential to help him.

First, Jason joined a boxing club when he was ten. For many the discipline of boxing has provided a way out from a life of crime and violence, and the start looked promising for Jason. He boxed there for about two and a half years. But it didn't channel his energies positively. 'I had to leave there because I beat one of the kids up and all the other kids turned against me. They chased me out of there really. So that was the end of that.'

Second, Jason got a job doing a paper round – a rite of passage for many British youngsters. In theory this was a way of learning responsibility, self-discipline and the importance of hard work – or in Jason's case it became a way of 'earning' some extra money by stealing from his customers. 'I started a paper round when I was about eleven – but I used that to find some opportunities to do some robbing. Opportunistic stuff – I weren't the best thief in the world! I was always looking for a pound note.'

The primary school years, from age four to eleven, should be a time of relative carefree innocence. But for Jason, drinking, violence and crime had already become part of his everyday life. It was unlikely that his behaviour would improve as he moved on to high school and the challenges of adolescence. In fact, it deteriorated.

Although education had never been important, schooling now slid even further down Jason's list of priorities. From the start Jason's attendance at high school was patchy. When he did bother to turn up, he was always looking for a fight. Even though he was one of the younger kids, he would happily fight anyone. 'I was always wanting to fight people – all through school. It was a massive thing. Any age. I didn't care. Sometimes I didn't even care if I won or lost. I just done it for the fun of it – the thrill. Sometimes I just liked being punched in the face. When you have been hurt so much, it's like a perverted way of feeling release from the world and the way it has treated you. I was very angry.' Jason's fighting was an outlet for the rage he felt towards the world. He also wanted to be tough for self-protection. 'I was on a mission to be tough. That was my mission in life. I didn't want anyone to ever hurt me again.'

Over the next few years Jason's bad habits became even more fixed and even more extreme. His behaviour became more violent and he began to use drugs. 'That was about when I got into puffing [cannabis]. We used to go robbing and just buy drugs. At twelve or thirteen I got onto the heavier stuff – speed. A few of the older lot started getting into heroin. Thank God I never got into that. Drugs and drinking were a big thing.'

Life at home was grim, so Jason spent as little time there as possible. That meant life was largely lived on the streets, and when it was cold and dark, anywhere warm would do. On Sunday evenings a service in a local church meant doors were open and the heating was on. Thirty-five years later Jason can still remember the welcome and patience shown to him by members of the church. 'I do remember, when I was about twelve, we was always out on the streets. We didn't like going home, because when you walked in the door, it all started right away. There was a church down Wrythe Lane – just past the girls' school. We used to go in there on a Sunday night. Just to keep warm really. Some of the other lads wanted to take the mick a bit. We ended up going to people's houses – Christian houses. They'd give us tea and biscuits, chatting and trying to tell us about God. And we were just trying to be a bit cheeky. Actually, we all kind of thought they was alright. They was just nice, welcoming people. They took a lot but still just showed that hospitality. I remember thinking, "I wonder if there is something in it?" It soon got drowned out by all the worldly stuff, all the bad stuff.' Years later, though, memories of that welcoming and kind group of Christians made it easier for Jason to walk into another church building and expect a warm welcome rather than a cold shoulder.

School was less welcoming. Jason attended less and less, and the teachers seemed relieved. 'I remember this teacher once. I was looking through this window into his classroom when I was about thirteen. He came out and swore at me, saying, "Armstrong, why don't you just get off the school grounds?" I went, "Yeah, whatever" and just walked off.' He was never followed up by truancy officers, and from then on attended school as little as possible. He reckoned he finished regularly attending school at thirteen.

So, lying about his age, Jason got work carrying crates of beer in the bars at racecourses. He was paid twenty to thirty pounds but worked out a way to earn far more. He organised a scam involving the cellarman and the barmaids, with himself as the middleman. They would steal crates of beer and sell them on to the punters at the races, splitting the profit three ways. That twenty to thirty pounds of legitimate wages were dwarfed by a regular two to three hundred pounds a day – sometimes as much as five hundred – he was earning on the side. 'I was quite popular at the time because I had loads of dough. I couldn't take it all home, coz they would be, "Where did you get all that from?" So I'd be spending it on drink and drugs with the lads. It was just drink and drugs all the way through high school really. Just drink and drugs.'

When he did occasionally turn up at school, it was still to fight rather than to learn – and the fights were becoming more violent. Having fought several older boys individually, he then challenged two of them to fight him at the same time. 'I went up there and the two of them was waiting for me. I had one of these metal plum bombs – a big, round cylinder of metal. I thought if I used that I could take the first one out quick and then do the second one. They both come towards me. I let go of the metal thing at the first one and split his eye open, and then nutted him – then he's gone. Then I done the other one. I beat both of them up – that was the end of that. I just got a buzz from the violence – when you done two bigger lads than you, and used the tool as well. For me and the world I was living in, it was kill or be killed. My fighting just escalated. I wanted to be the hardest kid in the school. Out of school I was working on the races, robbing, taking drugs. That was my school life.'

CHAPTER 4

Jason's school life ended for good when he was fifteen. He reckons he had only been in school for about a third of the statutory school days for the previous few years. Finally the teachers had had enough. 'They just told me to go.' So he went.

It was time for a 'proper' job. He joined his older brother, Lee, working in a double-glazing factory. At first the money was really disappointing after the easy money at the racecourses. 'It was rubbish money at the start at sixty quid a week, but after about six months they changed everything. I was quite fast at putting in the glass and doing the beading, and they changed the system there to a pound a pane, so my wages went up from sixty quid a week to about eleven hundred.'

He was earning good money honestly, but that didn't mean he spent it wisely. 'I had loads of money to burn, so I was out doing drugs and drinking every weekend, and one or two nights during the week as well.' He now looked old enough to be served in pubs. The violence moved from the playground to the bar, and also to the football ground. In an era of football hooliganism, violence before, during or after the match was all part of the match-day experience. 'I was about sixteen. We'd go to the football, Chelsea, and we used to get drunk there all the time. Sometimes there would be fights. Not too much really, but if it did happen, we didn't mind. There was football hooligans who used to go looking for it all the time.'

It was around this time that Jason first got seriously injured in a fight. 'I was seventeen the first time I got stabbed in my shoulder, cut, down there in Croydon. I fell out with this other lad and turned my back on him, and he just cut me down the back. I never saw him again so that's that.' His dad was not impressed. 'He punched me straight in the back of the head as I was sitting in this chair. I've jumped up asking, "What're you doing?" and he goes, "You keep fighting. I've heard about you fighting down at the pubs" and all that. So we started having a little bit of an argument.'

By this time Jason would have stood a good chance if he had chosen to fight. He was young, tough and fit. His dad was drunk. But something kept him from hitting back. 'The reason I wanted to be good at fighting was so I could beat him up. That was my initial goal. I wanted to do him, because he hurt my mum. But as it got later in life, I just couldn't bring myself to hit him really – I just didn't think it was right. It's your dad, you know what I mean? And he started changing as he got older. A lot of people would say don't forgive, but obviously now I know you should forgive, and I'm glad I did because you don't get nothing out of hurting your family really. So I walked out. I never went home again. That was it. I went and stayed with me nan.'

Jason might have moved out of the family home, but soon he was working for the family business. After eighteen months at the glass factory, he was made redundant, and there was work going in his dad's (legit) building firm. There was still time for less legitimate, money-making activities. And, despite being kicked out of home and being badly injured, there was still always time for drink, drugs and fighting.

The lack of a permanent home, his hatred of violence towards women and his willingness to use his fists led to his first significant relationship. 'When I was seventeen, I've got with S. She was ten or eleven years older than me at the time.' The age gap might have been unusual, but the way the relationship started was even more so. 'I was in the pub and she's there with her eight-year-old son and the bloke she's with at the time. They was arguing in the pub and he just knocked her spark out. And see, I remember my mum with my dad. I don't like women being hit by men. So I went over and knocked him out, and he's gone off in a car.'

When S came to, she asked Jason to see her home, just in case her ex turned up. 'So I took her home, and as we got in there, he's come out with a knife and stabbed her – she got cut quite badly on her hand. Then he's gone for me and goes for the little boy. So I grab the little boy and run down the stairs, and he's chasing me with this big knife. I got away and then the police turn up. He got nicked.' It was hardly love's young dream, but Jason stayed. Six months into that relationship she got pregnant.

You might expect that an eighteen-year-old in an unplanned relationship with an older woman would have been horrified by this equally unplanned pregnancy. You would be wrong. Jason told his mum, who insisted he told his dad, though they hadn't spoken for over a year. 'He said I had to get rid of it. Those were his first words. I didn't think that was right, so Kellie was born.'

A commitment of loyalty to friends, and also protecting women and children, were hardwired into Jason's DNA. With a volatile partner with a drink problem and a small daughter to look after, it could be hard to know who to protect and how. Once Jason believed he was protecting his family from a burglar, only to discover too late that the violent night-time attacker was his drunken girlfriend coming back from a night out. 'There's a porcelain lamp by the bed and she just smashed it over my head, and there was glass everywhere. Of course, I've jumped up, thinking it's a burglar. I got her on the floor and jumped on top of her, and weighed in what I thought was a burglar – and it was her! I said, "What you doing?" There's glass all over me and the baby. I just dragged her down the stairs and out the door.'

Sometimes he tried to protect S from herself. 'There was another occasion when she's drunk and got in the car. I said, "You ain't going off in the car," and I sat on the bonnet. So she just went off up the road, going about forty or fifty miles an hour. She stands on the anchors, and I've just gone flying – rolling, rolling, rolling. When I come to, I have a windscreen wiper in each hand – they come flying off, which I didn't even realise. It was quite funny, but then she tried to run me over. She was a bit crazy. That was our relationship.' Incredibly they stayed together six years.

Jason's domestic life was chaotic. His social life was no better. Even the 'good lads' on the estate would have been the 'bad lads' in most communities. 'I had two sets of friends. There were the friends who were half decent; they liked a bit of a fight, drugs, drink – pretty standard for council estate lads. There were the other friends who were really quite naughty.' 'Naughty' refers not to a badly behaved child but to friends who stabbed over a hundred people each and who would use knives with almost no provocation. In that company Jason was the voice of reason. He reckons that he was actually a good influence on some of his mates. 'Many times people may not have noticed, but I saved people from being seriously hurt. Sometimes I would just go, "Woah, just put the blades away. There's no need to get too heavy about it."'

Jason used to keep his friends separate. 'If one set of friends saw me talking to the other, they would go, "What are you talking to them for?" But I thought, "I get on with them as well. They are my mates as well. I've known them for a long time."' Of Jason's group of five close childhood friends, three are now dead from violence or drugs, and one is serving a life sentence in prison. Jason may have been the more reasonable one among them, but his moral standards were shockingly low.

That Jason had any moral compass at all is surprising. He now credits God with the fact that he did have some sort of morals. 'I had more morals than some, and less than others. I was sort of middle of the road. Whether that comes from the bits of church or because God puts morality in us, God was at work.' Jason's experiences of church included the occasional school assembly that he happened to attend, as well as the generous welcome of the church down the road to a bunch of scruffy, disrespectful kids on Sunday evenings. Black-and-white Bible epics on TV, like Charlton Heston's epic about Moses, also taught him a bit about God. 'In my house, my dad used to like all those old, big, Christian films. I remember even him telling me about them – how this is about Jesus, who is God. I don't know what his belief was. I don't think he had any to be honest, but he used to like watching the films.' But how could a totally morally perfect and fair God possibly have anything to do with someone like Jason?

CHAPTER 5

Given the company Jason kept and the lifestyle he lived, it is remarkable how little time he spent in prison. 'I had a few nickings for thieving and that in the teenage years. I was pretty lucky on the fighting front. I got away with it most of the time. I used to knock people out and just go out the back door. I didn't hang about.'

Even when he was arrested, he got off lightly. 'I was in the pub, and the landlord said to me, "You've had enough." I said, "Who are you telling, 'I've had enough?' I'll tell you when I've had enough." So I knocked him out. And I threw a glass at his head as well. But I missed his head – luckily enough, because otherwise I would have been in a lot more trouble. I had to peg it, and I see the old bill coming. So the only thing I could do was step into a phone box and start using the phone to try and hide myself. They got me! That's the only time I've ever gone quietly, coz I was trying to say, "I don't know what you are talking about." I just got a fine for that. Not too bad.'

Over the next few years, he came up in front of the same magistrate four or five times. They got to know each other quite well, and even developed a level of mutual respect. The magistrate was one of the very few authority figures who Jason didn't feel had let him down. His father, teachers and social workers, as well as the police, all thought he was beyond help and not worth bothering with. This particular magistrate saw some good in him and treated him as a human being. He once told him, 'Jason, you're a likeable chap, but you've got to learn to keep your hands to yourself.'

Jason's distrust of the police was fuelled further by another incident. He was charged with assault on a police officer, but felt the charge was totally unfair. Though he had resisted arrest after a brawl at a nightclub, when he had been accused of criminal damage, he insisted this had been nothing to do with him. Then at the police station the inspector called him names. It was this that led to Jason throwing a punch. 'All the other police jump on top of me. They rip all my clothes off. They was pinching me, punching me, pulling my nostrils, gouging my eyes, twisting my ears, digging me in the ribs. I was still trying to fight em. I haven't got a stitch of clothing on now. They got me in the cell and all hold me down – then counted one, two, three, jumped off me and ran out the door. So I jumped up and start kicking the door, coz I want a fight still. The morning, about eleven o'clock, they come and see me. On the way to the interview, they say to me, "Look, if you don't mention about us assaulting you, we won't say nothing about you hitting the inspector." I said, "That's fine. It's a deal." They was doing me for "fear or provocation of violence" – criminal damage. That was it, which I didn't think was too bad. Six weeks later I got charged through the post for assault on the inspector. I didn't even know they could do that! By that time all my bruises and that are gone. I thought that was a bit naughty.'

The case was adjourned three times before it eventually went to trial. Despite the delays, Jason never got round to getting a solicitor. He reckoned, wrongly, that he could get one on the day. 'I don't know why I didn't bother. I normally did. I went to court on this day and I thought it would just be another adjournment. So I spoke to the duty solicitor. He said, "It's going to trial today in courtroom two. I can't help you. I don't know anything about the case. It starts in five minutes."' Jason was left with no other option than to represent himself. He had obviously paid more attention to fictional courtroom dramas on TV than to actual procedures during his previous court hearings.

The same magistrate was on the bench that day. He tried to be helpful, but struggled to contain Jason's inner Perry Mason. 'So I go into court and it's the same magistrate again. I think he quite liked me really. He gives me a pen and paper and says, "When people are being questioned, you just sit there. And if there's something you don't agree with and you want to ask a question about, just write it down. So I'm sitting there, and this inspector's got up and he starts telling lies. I weren't happy – so I goes "No, no, no that didn't happen like that." The magistrate goes, "Look Jason, you're not allowed to get up until I tell you. Let him say his bit and you can speak to him after." He starts talking again and I goes, "No, no…" Three times this happens. In the end I got it, and I'm writing these things down. Then I had to get up and question him. I really laid it on a bit thick if I'm honest. He did not like it at all when I questioned him! "I put it to you, inspector…" He was going red in the face. The fear or provocation of violence was dropped. Criminal damage was dropped. I just got the assault on him, and I had to pay some damages. About three hundred quid. That was it. I done alright really.'

Again Jason got off lightly – he managed to get away with a fine for that assault. But the next time he was caught, he was not so lucky. When he knocked out another pub landlord who refused to serve him any more drinks, he was arrested. If Jason's cheek and charm had worked in his favour with the previous magistrate, it failed this time – and his explosive temper sealed the deal. 'I was offered community service. I spoke to my probation officer, and she said, "One hundred and eighty hours." I went, "Nah! I'm not doing one hundred and eighty hours." She went, "One sixty?" I went, "No." "One twenty?"' In the end Jason somehow got the hours down to eighty, or so he thought. 'When we got to court, she said one sixty again. I looked at the judge and said, "Nah." He said, "Do you accept this?" And I said, "No, I don't!" "What? You'll have to go to prison." "OK, I'll go to prison then." They went out and came back, and gave me three or four months.

I said, "How does that work out? I should be getting ten days if it was one hundred and sixty hours!" Because I was shouting and arguing, they just said, "Take him down." I was fuming.'

This was Jason's first time in prison. He shared a cell with one of his best mates, and it was a relatively easy experience. 'I did that first bit of bird at High Down, a local prison. It was quite a new prison then, not long open – about a year or so. They were still finding their feet there as well. Me and my mate Dave was in a cell together. We was just puffing all the time really. We were just having a party. They even forgot to lock our door one day. We was out on the landing, kicking everyone's doors, mucking about, winding everyone up. They didn't realise they had left us open. Crazy! We had a great day. We had a bit of a laugh and a joke in there.'

Jason's time in prison coincided with a time of tension between rival local gangs – in particular between Jason's mate Dave and another man who drank in the same pub. 'Before I went in that time, there was some ongoings with this geezer, T, from the pub. He was quite a naughty fella as well. Bearing in mind we were early twenties, he was in his thirties. He was quite a handful – about six foot four, twenty stone.' As Jason's mate Dave was already in prison, T thought he could 'slag him off' with impunity. But while Dave might have been locked up, his brother told him about the insults. Jason was able to fill in the details. Jason knew that Dave would never let the insults go unpunished.

Dave and Jason were let out of prison just a few days apart. On the day Jason got out, T and Dave had a fight – 'a straightener' – which ended up 'fifty-fifty'. Dave was only five foot five, but he was a good fighter. After that, T went back in the pub, where he had a few lines (of cocaine) and a drink. When he came out, he was ready for more action. 'Dave knew he was gonna come back. He's gone and got his blade and put it down his shorts, so he was ready for him. When T come back out, they started having it again and Dave stabbed T in the back. He lost a kidney.'

Things escalated from there. Dave and a friend planned to finish off T for good – they had a shotgun buried in Dave's garden. They expected Jason to help. 'Dave was trying to get hold of me. They couldn't – not many people had mobiles back then. They were ringing pubs, but I weren't in the pub.'

In fact Jason was in church. 'I look back at the times in my life and I see where I could have died or could have been involved in something really bad. I'm sure God used to put blockers in the way. I was supposed to go with two of my good mates to shoot someone and cut his throat. Ironically I was in a christening when they was trying to get hold of me to do him!'

Dave and his friend, James, went ahead without Jason. T was shot, his throat was cut and he was stabbed in the face. Fifteen minutes after Jason came out of church, he got a phone call from them saying, 'We was trying to get hold of you. We done it. Can you check and see if he is still alive?' He was – just. Jason arrived in time to see the paramedics working hard to save his life.

His friends were shocked and disappointed to hear that T was still alive. They laid low for a few weeks, going off to Manchester, because the gunpowder residue from firing the shotgun would be detectable for up to two weeks. 'Then they come back, and we met up at the safe house – someone's flat that was lent to them above the shops in the high street. They was public enemy number one – everyone was after them.' Just out of prison, having apparently got away with a violent assault, which could have led to a significant custodial sentence, and having avoided retaliation from the victim's gang, common sense would have suggested keeping out of trouble for a while. Common sense was in short supply.

While Dave and his friend were still using the safe house, Jason joined them for a night out. 'They didn't care if they was caught. The old bill was looking for them everywhere. They was raiding loads of houses and going mad for em. We went out for a drink. There was a big group of lads in there, about twenty of them. There was just us three. James just loves a fight, just looking for trouble. I'm saying, "Just calm down." He jumps up and pulls out a samurai sword that was down his trousers. He was going to start doing people. I grabbed his arm. I said, "Just leave it. They ain't doing nothing to you, it's all in your mind." He was crazy.'

They moved on to a friendlier pub, the same pub where the attack on T had started and where they got a hero's welcome. 'They were sort of heroes because the other bloke was a horrible bully. Everyone loved it that they had done him.' It was also the first place the police would look for them, so after a couple of drinks, they called a taxi and moved on. 'I remember the cab driver saying, "Don't go in there boys. Someone got shot and stabbed there the other week" – not knowing that he had the two geezers that done it in his cab, which I thought was really funny at the time.'

Dave and James had got away with attempted murder. They thought they were invincible. 'It kind of made them go a little bit madder really.' Jason might have been more reasonable than some of his friends, but his life was still out of control – he was 'still fighting, drinking, taking drugs. You think you are happy when you are in that frame of mind and in that bad place – in that darkness – but you're not really. You only realise when you stop and think about your life. That's what keeps you going 100 miles an hour, so you never think about how bad your life is. I only see that now. I didn't see that then. I thought my life was great. I thought I was a bit of a chap – I had a little bit of money in my pocket.'

CHAPTER 6

One part of Jason's life was about to change for the better. His relationship with his girlfriend had never been stable. He loved and cared for Kellie, his little girl, but had never expected to be with her mum for as long as six years. The relationship ended after a group weekend at Butlin's holiday park. 'Loads of us went to Butlin's all together. Things with S, Kellie's mum, were on the down. It wasn't really going anywhere. S went home, and me and Lorna got talking and things. Nothing happened – but they thought it had. I walked her back to her room, but nothing happened.' When Jason came home, he was confronted by S: '"I know you went with her…" She had already packed my bags. I wanted a way out anyway, so I just grabbed my bags and went. I didn't argue. I went back to my nan's again.'

Lorna and Jason had known about each other for years. Lorna's uncle, who was only a few years older than her, was one of Jason's best mates. Lorna's and Jason's mothers had worked together and become close friends.

Jason's mother had even stayed with Lorna's family for a time, to escape the domestic abuse. Lorna remembers first meeting Jason. 'I didn't really know him that well. He used to come round to our house on Saturday mornings because he had ordered stuff from my mum's catalogue. We all used to chat then. I thought, "He's quite a nice bloke." It was his personality. He made me laugh. I was very close to my uncle Paul, because he actually lived with us. I thought if Jason is good friends with Paul, and Paul is a decent bloke, then he must be a good person as well.'

It wasn't long before Lorna realised that Jason was less of a 'good person' than she had thought. As Jason puts it, 'One of the first times I was out with her, there was some geezer in there chatting her up. I just left her talking to him, I thought she could handle herself. She comes up to me and says, "Keep him away from me, he's driving me mad." I goes, "Listen to me, mate, she doesn't want to talk to you anymore. Go away." He pushed me. He says, "Get away from her – she's mine!" He was with about twenty blokes. It was only me and Lorna – I didn't know anyone else in there that night. These twenty blokes surrounded me. I says to Lorna, "Just go. I'm gonna do em." I broke a couple of bottles and said, "Come on then, let's have it." In my mind I just do a few and don't care if they do me. It's death before dishonour – it's pathetic, I know. That's the way your brain is made up – never give in, never lose. They ended up not wanting it, when they see me with the tools and that. So I managed to walk out. The bouncers come up as well. So, I walked out with Lorna.'

It was hardly a perfect first date, but at least no one had been hurt – yet. 'We was walking down slowly, chatting. We got to the bridge and he's following us. He's running up and shouting, "Leave her alone – she's mine." He must have been off his head. He's took his shirt off. He's coming towards me. So I just hit him. Bang, knocked him spark out. I really weighed him in. Severely. I broke his face completely. Lorna was pretty disgusted really at the level of violence. I was stamping on his face, jumping on it. I lost it. That's the level that was in there. I knew that she didn't like that. I felt bad about that, coz she's a decent woman.'

Lorna may have been disgusted, but she was also pleased that Jason had protected her from unwanted attention. She stuck with him. 'I did know that he liked a fight, but I didn't really know how violent he could be. I think coming from a council estate, men did fight in pubs, so I didn't really think much of it at the time. I did shout at him to stop because I thought he was going over the top – I don't come from a violent family, not even arguments really. I'm not used to that. I don't know if maybe I was a little bit impressed – I knew he could protect me.'

If Lorna was impressed by Jason's violence, Jason was overwhelmed by Lorna's goodness. 'People say, "What's the best part of me?" I say it's Lorna. When I look back at the work God's done in my life, one of the biggest things he's done is put us together. Because she really is a decent person. She helps people. She really cares about people. She's genuinely a good person. She never broke the law. When we first got together, I didn't really know how to love. Her family is very close. They always want to see each other, talk to each other on the phone. My family's nothing like that. We don't care. If one of us died tomorrow, we'd probably say, "That's another one gone."'

Jason's violence soon caused problems for his new relationship. After just a few months together, another fight led to a conviction for grievous bodily harm with intent, and a five-and-a-half-year prison sentence. Jason had been drinking all day before going round to Lorna's home. Her family, including her five-year-old brother, were all going to a party. Jason, already drunk, tagged along. It was unlikely to end well. He admits he was showing off and winding up the other guests. Those who knew him just put up with his behaviour. Those who didn't had soon had enough. 'I was a bit drunk, dancing around – there was people there who didn't know me who took offence at that. It kicked off basically at the end of the night.' Initially Lorna's dad was attacked, but it was when Jason got involved that it turned nasty.

From previous fights Jason had learnt that hurting one person very badly was usually enough to make the others back off. It worked, but not before he had almost killed a man. 'I picked up a bottle and slashed him across the face. Then I grabbed his hair and done him in the face with a champagne flute which broke. I was left with the stem, and I stabbed him in the neck three times. Someone grabbed my back, and I stabbed them in the leg and the hand. I did someone else in the arm I think, but they didn't press charges. I missed his jugular by three millimetres apparently. That would have killed him. It stopped the fight though.'

In the past Jason had just walked away from fights. Not this time. 'I went to go out the fire exit way to get away. It was chained up and locked. I had the hump because they had chained up the fire exit. I thought, "This ain't right!" See the mentality? It's crazy! That's what I had the hump about, not that I had just cut someone and nearly killed them.' Cut off from his usual way out, surrounded by his victim's friends and with the police on the way, escape was unlikely. 'I thought I'd go out the front door. There was about thirty or forty of them all shouting and screaming. The police just come and grab hold of me.'

Despite, or perhaps because of the prospect of a long prison sentence, Jason and Lorna got engaged shortly before the trial. Jason sees Lorna as a God-given gift to protect him from his worst instincts. That was certainly the case the night of their engagement party. The party was at Lorna's parents' house, but the happy couple had met up with friends beforehand at the pub. Jason and Lorna left for the party with plans for the others to meet them later. 'They didn't make it because Dave and Paul ended up having a fight and someone nearly got killed. Dave got jumped outside when he was having a fag. Paul, his little brother, come out, sees Dave getting done, goes and gets a club hammer, and hit the geezer in the back of the head. When he was on the floor, he smashed him on the forehead with it – three times, as hard as he could. He shattered his skull. Nearly killed him. They didn't make it to the party.'

Being with Lorna had prevented Jason from being caught up in his friends' increasingly violent behaviour.

Being with Lorna also gave him a cast-iron alibi. 'Next day the police are round my house and questioning me about it, coz I was seen with them at the pub. They wanted names. That was all I needed when I was going to court in three days for GBH myself.' Jason's trial lasted four days, and ended with him being sentenced to five years and five months for GBH with intent. Had he been involved in the latest attack, he could have got life.

Looking back, Jason recognises God's hand on his life many years before he showed any interest in spiritual matters himself. God is God and is at work in his world whether we believe in him or not. God is God and cares about us, whether we care about him or not.

CHAPTER 7

Jason had been in prison before, but only for a few months. How would he cope with such a long stretch? Would Lorna wait for him? Could he trust her to be faithful? It was also the middle of winter when Jason began his sentence. 'It was a nightmare really. I was put in a cell. It was January, so it was freezing cold. One window was hanging off. It was just bars there, so there was wind blowing through. They give me this little sheet and this little blanket, with holes in. I was freezing! It was such a depressing night. All my other stuff was down at reception, so I had nothing – I was in the holding cell coming from court, coz I knew I was going down.' The first days were tough. 'I just thought, "Oh no, this is it. I've got four to five years of this." Then you just get into it. The worst I remember was when I was in the cell one afternoon, about three to four days in. I was trying to find my feet, find my way – I'd only done three months before that. I was in my cell and this little bit of paper comes under the door. It had the release date – how many days you've got to serve. We are in January 1996 and my release date was August 1999.' Sentences served are always less than the sentence given, but for a young man of just twenty-six, three and a half years seemed like a lifetime.

He soon realised that the only way to get through was to just 'get on with it'. 'You get people in there who fight the system, carry on being Charlie Big Spuds and all that. It's just pointless. You can't win. You don't beat the system.' The key thing was not to have the sentence extended. 'I know a lot of people who have done a lot of prison, just because they didn't get their head down. You know, you are no good to no one in there. So I try to keep my head down in there most of the time. You just settle in.' In the end he found his first six months comparatively easy.

He settled into a routine. He went to the gym regularly. 'I used to go to the gym a lot. I thought I might as well get fit and healthy.' He also settled into a routine of using, buying and selling drugs. Drugs had made his previous stay in prison more manageable, so this time he had come prepared. He smuggled in some cannabis and sleeping pills. Had he been caught, he would have had an extra eighteen months added to his sentence.

When he ran out, more drugs were readily available. 'I had a geezer, Errol, who lived above me, and he was the wing drug dealer.' Errol's method for getting drugs to people was fairly creative – it involved a little Marvel tin and a bed blanket, which would be unravelled to make a long string of wool. 'Some of them are so good at it they can swing it round with batteries on and even get to other wings. They can hit a window, and someone would get a parcel. It's crazy. There are some right clever people in there. I used to get stoned pretty much every night.' Jason was also dealing heroin. It was easier to hide than other drugs and could be traded for cannabis. 'It was just to get some puff for me. It's just a currency.'

Hiding heroin didn't cause any problems until Jason's younger brother, Kevin, was admitted to the same prison. Jason asked for him to be put into his cell. 'But that was a bad mistake.' Jason was unaware that his brother was using heroin. He bagged up the drugs as usual, showed his brother where they were hidden and went off to his education session, unknowingly leaving an addict in charge of the deals. Later that day a customer came to the cell. 'I'm trying to find the stuff and saying, "Where is it?" And my brother's pretending to look with me. I'm thinking, "This ain't right!" The gear had gone, he's taken everything.' Kevin tried to deny everything. Soon punches were being thrown. 'He's trying to throw one at me, so we've started fighting. Somehow he's biting my back, so I've just done him with the chair leg over his head and then nutted him. But he's pressed the buzzer, so all the screws are come running down.'

Jason was furious. His thieving, drug-using younger brother was calling the guards for help, which would inevitably lead to punishment and constraints on his drug business. 'This isn't like at home, calling mum or dad or something – this is serious. So they come and there's chairs and tables all over the cell. It's like bedlam. And I'm standing by the door saying, "It's all right guv, it's nothing. He just pressed the buzzer accidentally" – so they wouldn't look into the cell.' Incredibly the guards believed Jason's explanation. 'They've swallowed it. They've gone away and we've tidied up.'

Although his brother was in prison for only a few more days, Kevin's short stay had a further impact on Jason. He had been stealing from other dealers too. If the money was not paid back, they threatened to have Kevin beaten up, or worse. 'He took loads of gear off some of the naughty people on the wing, and they come to me wanting their money, otherwise they's going to do him. Obviously I couldn't let them do him coz he's my brother. I had to pay the debt, which was a bit of a nightmare. I had to get money sent in. It was hard work.'

Jason was always loyal to his family, however badly he was treated. It was not the last time that Kevin joined him inside. 'He come back again when I was about halfway through my sentence. He got four years. He had robbed my wife Lorna's cousin on a motorbike at knife point. He took his money when he was delivering pizzas. That was embarrassing! Crazy innit?'

But Lorna wasn't his wife yet. Unsurprisingly a lot of relationships break down in prison. Lorna and Jason might have just got engaged, but she was only twenty-two years old. Would she really wait for him? 'We had only been together a year and she said she was going to wait for me. That was in the August before I went away. I said,

"You can't just say things like that, because if you do, I'll expect you to do it." She did! Talk about "prove yourself". She used to send money in. She was always there on visits – never missed one. I think she had it harder than me in some ways. I see a picture her mum sent me once – she was sitting there just looking really down.'

For Lorna, the decision to wait for Jason was fairly simple. 'I never considered not sticking with him. I couldn't walk away. I didn't want to walk away really. I felt a bit guilty coz obviously I was still going out with friends a lot of the time and going round to his mum's. But I had good friends and family behind me.' That doesn't mean that maintaining their relationship was easy. 'At the start you just get half-hour visits every couple of weeks, I think it was. It was hard not seeing each other. You look forward to the phone calls.' There were also misunderstandings. One night Lorna had gone out with Jason's sister, then went back to the home of one of Jason's friends with another man. They didn't stay long, but when Jason heard about it, he was furious. 'He got quite jealous. We had this really big row over it. I just thought, being in there, he's in this little bubble. He's just got time to think all the time. Just one little thing can be blown out of all proportion. It made me realise what it was like for him.'

Lorna didn't just work hard to keep her relationship with Jason going, she also made sure that he saw his daughter regularly. 'On Saturdays I took Kellie up. I think it was an hour the visits. I think she used to think it was quite fun really because they had a little corner with toys in. She'd get Mars bars and coke and see her dad.' Lorna was also supporting, and being supported by, Jason's mum, who had experience of her husband and two of her sons being in prison. 'His mum was really good at that time. She had been through it with his dad. I think that really brought me closer to his mum at that time as well.'

Lorna and Jason's mum might have made his life in prison more bearable, but his dad made it less so. A prison officer had seen Jason's father in the pub and threatened to 'do' Jason while he was on duty. 'He said he was going to do me to my dad, which he shouldn't have said, and my dad stabbed him twice in the belly. They caught him in the Chinese, but they didn't find him with the knife.' Some of Jason's dad's gangster friends put pressure on the officer to retract the charges. Jason reckons that some of the 'screws' treated him worse as a result. 'A few of them were funny towards me. It was only because of that, no doubt.'

There were other reasons that the prison officers might have acted strange towards Jason. He might have planned to just keep his head down and do his time, but life in prison was boring, so he took any opportunity for a bit of fun. 'I remember once Dave came for a visit, and I was up on the top landing where the screws never went much. He'd got, I think, six to eight grammes of Charlie [cocaine] and thirty ecstasy pills. We was all in my cell, about fifteen of us, having a party, and it was mental. It was a great night. I just remember all through the night everyone just got music blaring, and the screw knocking on the cell saying, "Turn the music down."'

The next day, coming down from the drugs high, and suffering from sleep deprivation, they were in no mood for cooperation. 'We was out in the exercise yard and there's about ten of us in a circle. Someone said, "Listen, if they tell us to go in, we're just not having it. We ain't going in. Stand firm. We will stay together."' Ten hungover prisoners were never going to be able to hold out for long once the guards realised what was happening. 'So they press the buzzer. There's about twenty or thirty screws now. Dogs are right by the area. They are being held back and barking. They're prison dogs – not police dogs. They're killer dogs, and they go for you.' Jason might have had the party in his cell with drugs provided by his friend, but he wasn't the ringleader of this mini strike. He would have been very happy to just meekly return to his cell – but he didn't want to be the first to give in. 'The guy's going, "Stand firm! Stand firm!" So we're sitting at their feet, and I'm thinking, "Someone get up please!" Someone, I don't really know who, ends up getting up, and you can just see the relief on everyone's face cause no one else is willing to. So we got out of that one. But yeah, they weren't happy, the screws.'

One of the prison staff did treat Jason with compassion and understanding – the chaplain. After a family tragedy, he arranged for Lorna to have a private visit in the chapel. Although the chaplain was officially present, he did allow them some time alone. Lorna appreciated the gesture and reckons this small act of kindness had an impact on Jason. 'The chaplain was there as well, but he sort of went off and made a cup of tea for us. Jason did have an experience of the chaplain, but he wasn't interested in God at that time, I don't think. All those little things make a difference.'

After about a year, Jason was sent to a Category C prison, for prisoners who can't be trusted in an open prison, but who are considered unlikely to try and escape. There was a bit more freedom and time out of the cell, even opportunities for work 'outside'. It might have been a different category of prison, but it was still filled with the same category of people. 'I was on C wing down in the dungeons in the basement bit. It's dodgy around there. There were a lot of thieves – people going in the cells and that and nicking stuff.' Quite soon he got moved to another cell, in another wing of the prison, and settled in to complete his sentence. Ideally he would have spent his time in the gym and playing badminton – 'I was good at badminton as it goes.' Generally his time there was uneventful, except for one incident that could have extended his sentence considerably – and which made him spend his final months there in a state of anxiety.

Jason befriended a much older prisoner, who shared mutual friends. It appears that he was developing dementia. He started telling people that Jason had accused him of being a sex offender. 'He lost the plot and thought I was telling people he was a nonce. I never done it. I found out that he said he was gonna do me.' Jason tried to talk to him, but he was brushed off. '"Did you tell people I'm calling you a nonce?" "Nah – it's all sweet, Jason." But I could see in his eyes the hate and all that.' A couple of days later, the old man was found with his throat cut in his cell, with a note naming Jason, and two other prisoners in their seventies, as the culprits. He was still alive, but only just. His note had said that Jason had held him down with two accomplices. It was that detail that got Jason off the hook. Jason was a much bigger, younger man, who spent most of his time in the gym. The idea that he had needed to be helped by two pensioners was laughable. Had the assault been pinned on Jason, he would have had another ten years added to his sentence just a few months before his release date.

It was not over for Jason yet because they let his accuser back in the prison. 'I said to the governor, "What are you letting him back for? He obviously thinks it's me. He might try and get me now." That's what they wanted to happen really. He never did. What he did do was abscond. I found out that when he absconded, he told a few people he's gonna get his brothers and get me when I was on day release. He said to people, "When Jason's on outside work, we're going to run him over and kill him."' Jason was given a licence to work outside of prison, and used to help out at an old people's home. But now he was really worried, so took precautions. 'I've got my solicitor in, and he left me a cosh down in the bottom of the road. A telescopic one. He was dodgy as anything – that's why I used him! I just drive down the bottom of the road to get the cosh, put it in the side of my trousers or in this little rucksack, and drive off to the old people's home. But when I was driving, I kept looking behind me. It was terrifying for a little while there. Nothing ever happened.'

Eventually Jason finished his prison sentence. 'I got through my sentence. End up getting out in July 98 in the end. I did two years eight months. I was on licence for eighteen months. Signed on at probation and all that. You've got to be really careful at that time or they'll just call you back.'

When he was in prison Jason had promised Lorna that he would not get into trouble again. 'I said to her, "If you wait for me, I'll lose weight and I'll start behaving myself." Unfortunately, I didn't behave myself fully. I did lose a lot of weight. I come out of prison really trim. I was thirteen stone four. I was benching like a hundred and sixty kilos, which is about three hundred and twenty-five pounds. I was pretty strong – big biceps and triceps. She enjoyed that time with me!' Lorna had waited, and Jason wanted to honour his promise. 'When I come out, I did want to change. I did try.'

Lorna had made a real difference to Jason's life. 'She's always been a rock in my life. I would have definitely been dead, or doing life, if it wasn't for Lorna, because I honestly believe that she's the one God put in my life to stop me from stepping over that line too far. I believe that because she made me think about what I'm doing. She brought a different element. I cared. Before I didn't care what I was doing. I didn't care if I lived or died. It didn't bother me. But with her I started to care. But there was always conflict between the good me and the bad me. She was the one who would let the good side win a lot of the time, because I'd listen to her.'

God may have put Lorna in Jason's life, but he needed God himself, not just Lorna, if he was really going to change. The kind of radical transformation Jason needed could never be brought about by good intentions or even hard work.

CHAPTER 8

Initially things looked up once Jason left prison and he kept out of serious trouble for a while. 'Things were quieter, and I was that bit older as well. We took Kellie to Alton Towers for her tenth birthday which was nice – the year after I got out. We had a great time.' But he still wasn't a model partner. 'I don't really know how Lorna put up with all the rubbish she's put up with over the years. I usually had four nights a week out drinking, fighting, snorting.'

Jason had gone back to working for the family building firm when he came out of prison, but quite soon trouble hit. Jason had never liked his father's business partner. 'He was a horrible man. He's like a bulldog chewing a wasp. He's just bad to the bone.' Recently out of prison, and fighting fit, Jason refused to be bullied. When he was hit, he hit back. At first Jason's father tried to keep the peace for the sake of the business, but some of his gangster friends took Jason's side and sent two heavies to the pub to finish 'the bulldog' off. Jason was relieved that the business partner had left already, pretty sure that they would have killed him. That didn't stop Jason turning up to a meeting the next day ready to fight. 'I still wanted to get him. The next day I'm still fuming. My dad's going to have a meeting with him – him and his boy, and me and my dad. My dad didn't know, but I had a big blade down the back of my trousers, and I was going to do him.' Once again his dad calmed down the situation, but the partnership was doomed. If Jason had had his way, the partnership would have ended years earlier. Jason wasn't sad to see the partner go. But at first the business struggled. 'I was working for nothing really, twelve-hour days for two years to save the business.'

And soon enough Jason was in trouble again, but of a different kind. It started out in a predictable way – a fight in a pub. Jason might have been trying to behave for Lorna's sake, but even she was not enough to counter the influence of drink, drugs and his explosive temper. 'It was in 2000 when I was thirty-one. I'd been out a couple of years and was in a pub one night. There was these three geezers in the pub. A few of us had been in there all day, drinking, taking Charlie and drinking away. I was playing darts in the corner and had a little altercation with these lads. They were really bolshy, just out for trouble. I found out afterwards they was quite naughty people. Then my mate has nicked one of their hats, asking for a light or something, having a laugh. These people were in a different league. My mates didn't mind a fight but they weren't ready for big knives and all that. I see the geezer pull out a big knife with a wooden handle – a long blade that went to a point. I went, "He's got a blade." My mate's running forward, coz the geezer's gone to do him in the back. As I shouted, the geezer's turned to me. He come towards me. I smacked him a right hook. He's slung a knife. As I hit him, the knife's gone through my lower arm – the tip of it went right through and pulled back out. He was knocked out. He was slumped over in between the bar and this pier. I had him lovely, so I was just giving him uppercuts in the face. I picked him up by his hair and was smashing his face on the glass beer pump. Then I let him go coz everyone stopped me. Someone said, "What's the matter with your arm?" There's a big hole in my jumper and you could see through my arm.'

Despite being badly injured, Jason went on the attack. Once again the level of violence was extreme. 'Then I lost it. I picked him up from the floor and dragged him over to this pier with a mirror on it. I was just smashing his face in this mirror. After I threw him down I smashed a glass and ran over to stick it in his face. Then someone grabbed me and pulled me back just as I was about to do him. There was a copper standing just by the glass door, but he didn't come in because he was on his own.' Jason had got lucky. 'That would have been my second strike so I would have got life.'

Jason's injuries were so severe that he risked losing his arm. He had severed an artery and his ulnar nerve, as well as damaging tendons. In working life, he was a builder. In his social life, he was a fighter. It was possible that he would never work, or fight, again. Internal bleeding led to complications, and he needed an operation to relieve the pressure, but this had to be delayed because of the quantity of drugs in his system. 'I had compartment syndrome, which is a complication. So when I went into surgery, they said I might not have my arm when I came out. It's bleeding internally in the compartments. It felt like someone was tightening it up. The pressure built and built and built. They had to wait three hours before they could take me into surgery because I was coked up and drugged. I was there in pain for hours.'

He came out of the operating theatre still with both arms but needing further surgery at a specialist orthopaedic hospital. 'Then I got taken to Stanmore orthopaedic hospital with Lorna in an ambulance. The geezer who took me – the ambulance driver – I was in prison with! The first time I met him was in prison. The second time he's taking me to hospital in a private ambulance. Then I see him a year after that in the supermarket. By then he was an undertaker. I said, "I don't want to see you no more!"'

Jason was very grateful for the referral to Stanmore. His original surgeon knew that a world expert in operating on similar injuries was visiting from Sweden and referred Jason to him. 'It was really big of him to send me there. I was there for two to three days because of the swelling, and they took me down for the big op. He put the artery back together, and to mend the nerve he put this thin cord to encourage the nerve to grow along it. Apparently it only grows a millimetre a year. By the time it's grown back I'll be long gone.' Jason was in hospital for a further three weeks on strong painkillers. He had experience of many different illegal drugs over the years, but they had not prepared him for his reaction to morphine. 'I had been on it for four or five days and I came up with this really bad rash on my legs, so they had to take me off that. I was seeing things as well. I was seeing black things coming out the walls and all sorts – really weird. It doesn't really kill the pain, but it takes you somewhere else. You're not with it.' He was sent home, but after a couple of days was back in with an infection and the wound 'smelling like an old sock!'

Eventually the swelling reduced, and the wound was stitched up, but Jason still faced months of physiotherapy and painful exercises if there was to be any chance of regaining the use of his arm. 'I had physio for ten months. I kept going to this specialist orthopaedic clinic in London.' Seeing other patients motivated him to take his treatment seriously. 'There were other people in there and their injuries weren't as bad as mine, but all of them had these purple arms doing nothing.' Jason's response to difficulty had always been to fight rather than give in. He adopted the same approach to his recovery. 'I was working hard, doing all the exercises. In tears sometimes with pain. And luckily enough I had Lorna massaging me every day. That helped as well. I really wanted my right arm back. My life's ruined without that. I worked hard, a lot of tears, a lot of heartache.'

At the end of treatment, the Swedish surgeon was amazed at his progress compared to others in the clinic and wanted to know the secret of Jason's success. 'I said "I've worked hard to get it back. I've done all the exercises. There's been tears and heartache. I've kept going. I've kept trying." He said, "Do you mind waiting for half an hour and coming back in?" I thought that's the least I can do. I've gone back in there and there's about fifteen other doctors.' Jason was the model patient! He was an example of what could be achieved with enough determination, even after the most serious injury. He had been unable to work for ten months, but had used the time to make sure that he would be able to work again. He regained ninety percent of the movement in his right arm, although the feeling in two fingers never returned.

This would have been an ideal time for Jason to reassess his life. Previously drinking, drugs and fighting had led to a lengthy stay in prison. This time they had led to him almost being permanently disabled. Maybe now was the time to turn his life around and change his ways. Or maybe not. He started out with good intentions, as he had after his release from prison. 'After that I thought, "I've really got to calm down with the fighting."' That resolution was broken while he was still in recovery. 'About three months in, when it's still all bandaged up and I can't really use it, a couple of my mates had a bit of trouble down the estate. They've called me, but I don't know what I can do. I've only got me left hand. There's thirty of them! They was smacking me over the head. It was awful.' Even though Jason couldn't fight properly, his reputation was enough to scare the mob off. 'When they found out who they'd done, they all disappeared. They got away with it really.' He considered going after them 'tooled up' but thought better of it.

Wanting to stand by his mates, and the thrill of the fight, was more powerful than the fear of further damaging his arm. Good intentions would never be enough to change the habits of a lifetime. Another habit that could not be broken was Jason's drug use. In fact, unable to work and needing a new source of income, drug use led to drug dealing. More readily available drugs led to still more drug use. 'So I served up a bit of gear to help with a bit of money – though I didn't earn much because I was doing most of it. I was bored, not working myself. I was getting high on my own supply. That was a bit of a rough time. Lorna was not very happy with that again.'

Prison and serious injury had been God-given opportunities for Jason to change. While earlier he had been quite happy with his life, he could now see the impact his behaviour was having on his relationship with Lorna, but he was incapable of breaking old habits. Maybe he was now too old, and his character too established, for him to be able to start again. Maybe he would just mellow a bit with age – if he lived long enough.

CHAPTER 9

Jason was now in his thirties, in a stable relationship and with a young daughter. Despite lapses, his life seemed to be calming down. Jason reckons this was because he wasn't mixing with such a bad crowd – not because he had decided to mend his ways, but because so many of his friends were dead. 'I only had a couple of silly fights during my thirties. I was doing alright, not too bad. I clumped a few people, but nothing really heavy. Maybe that was because a lot of my mates had died – the real naughty ones.'

Jason's old friends may have been trouble, but he missed them. In his early teens Jason had decided not to use heroin. Friends who did, died young. The death of Dave, at thirty-three, particularly hurt Jason. 'Good mate of mine, Dave. I loved him. He was a proper geezer. He'd do anything for me. I'd do anything for him. We was close. I was best man at his wedding. I tried to help him with the drugs – he was on heroin. He'd come round when he was off it and we would play computer games. I'd try and keep him calm. I helped him as much as I could. I was gutted when he went.' Dave's brother Paul also died young – when he was only twenty-one. Given his behaviour, Jason seems surprised he lived so long. One time Paul turned up late to meet Jason. 'Paul's turned up in his little orange mini, forty minutes late. "Where was you?" "I had a row with some lorry driver in Purley. He was trying to be a bully and cut me up. He got out his car and put his hands on my bonnet and started having a go. So I just run over him. He was standing in front of my car – what was I supposed to do? It was like going over a big road hump." That was their mentality. I was always trying to keep them calm.'

Others in Jason's crowd were less missed. 'James, not so much. He was mental, too much. He was hard work. He always wanted to stab people. All the time. Shooting people as well. I did hear that a few people gave him some hooky gear on purpose coz he was causing too much trouble in the manor [neighbourhood]. I was told that by some of the heavies. Once he shot Julian in the Goat pub – shot him in the belly. Julian's dead now too. He got killed in Spain. He was a nice fella Julian, but drugs got him too. He was a good-looking lad – he used to train. They found him dead in an alley in Spain.'

Jason had experienced the deaths of more close friends than most people of his age. Death often causes us to consider the meaning of life and the possibility of what comes next. Jason felt vindicated by his early decision never to use heroin.

Some of the bad influences in Jason's life had gone. Lorna, a very positive influence, was still around. 'Me and Lorna was doing alright. Then I did probably the worst proposal ever. I was down the pub one night, and her friend Louise said, "Lorna'd like to get married." I said, "Would she?" So I rang Lorna and said, "Do you want to get married?" She said, "Yeah." So I said, "Let's do it." That was my proposal! Very romantic!' They had been together for nine years, and although they were engaged Jason had never considered marriage. His father's abusive behaviour towards his mother hadn't been a great example of marital bliss. Lorna's parents were happily married, and she had always dreamed of her own perfect white wedding in church. 'I come from a family that had got a good marriage. It's that commitment you make together. I didn't want to be with anyone else. For all of his faults, Jason is a good guy. I knew that he loved me, so why would I want someone else?'

Getting married in church meant marriage preparation meetings with the vicar and church attendance for several months – because the couple lived outside the parish boundaries of St Lawrence, where Lorna wanted to get married. Jason had to go to the meetings with the vicar but he refused to go to church, so Lorna went with her mum. The wedding was Lorna's dream day – despite dreadful weather. 'It was November. It was teeming down so we couldn't have no pictures outside. It was hammering down all day.' It was a great day for Jason too. 'I got married in 2003. I was thirty-four. Lorna was thirty. We got married at St Lawrence, because that was the church for Lorna. That was the one she felt close to. She had some faith because of her nan. She wanted a hundred percent church wedding with a white dress. She wanted to do it properly, then have a baby. That mattered to her. We got married and had a fantastic day. It was a great wedding.'

Lorna had her perfect wedding. The honeymoon was more Jason's style. 'I booked us to go to Barbados the next day at five in the morning. Which on reflection was silly. I should have left a day in between. We was just dying in the cab and on the flight. But when we got there, we had a great time. Although I did start nearly fighting the American marines!' Cocaine was cheap and plentiful, and Jason made the most of the opportunity. With drink and drugs in his system, he started taunting a couple of marines and they didn't like it. 'I was trying to fight them in the carpark. I remember the Barbadian cab driver saying, "Just get in the cab, man." Lorna was going, "Get in the car." We had a great time apart from that night.'

Lorna married Jason knowing what kind of man he was, and what kind of background he came from. Any hopes he would change once he was a married man were disappointed. 'I was still getting up to no good. Selling drugs, drinking. Still out about three or four nights a week. Still a bit bolshy. That was just normal to me really. I didn't know how to love. When you come from a difficult background, it's hard. Me and Lorna didn't row a lot, but we rowed more than we needed to. That's because of my attitude and the way I was – an alpha male who just talks down to everyone. Sometimes you don't even realise you are doing it. It's the way you have always been. And you're a bit bitter inside as well. And twisted because of the abuse – violent, physical and sexual. All them things in your head are still there and they don't go away. It turns you into the person you are. I didn't know there was any other way.' How did Lorna feel about this? 'She didn't really say a lot to be honest. She was just used to it. What I was and who I was. That being said, I'm sure she would have wanted me there more. When you are like that, you don't mean to be selfish, but you are.'

At least the business was flourishing. Although his dad was officially in charge, Jason was effectively running the operation. He had forty men working under him and the company was turning over nearly three million pounds a year. If he was to keep working, he needed to protect his hands, so most of the time he kept his fists to himself. 'Things were pretty quiet on the fighting side because I was injured anyway. My right hand is not as good as it was. It actually hurts if I hit anything with it. That's why I wear gloves when I'm working. It's all ultra-sensitive.'

Things settled into a predictable rut for a few years until another major family event happened. After a long wait and a difficult birth, Lorna's longed-for child was born – a daughter called Bo. Jason, the hard man, was softening. 'It was quite emotional. I had to turn away for a second coz I was all choked up. Bo started crying after about ten minutes and never stopped for about two years! She was quite a tough baby in that respect! Lorna done it well, her first child.' Lorna had continued to be close to Kellie, Jason's other daughter. They had a good relationship. Now Kellie was involved in the life of her little sister. 'She was excited as well. It was lovely.'

Lorna had had her traditional church wedding. Now she wanted their daughter, Bo, to be baptised. Lorna had been christened as a baby, and she wanted the same for her daughter. Baptism meant more preparation classes – this time in their home with a member of the church, Roy. 'I can't remember what he said. All I remember is him always praying with us. Jason just thought, "Nice old bloke – but he's talking rubbish." I would say, "Don't be nasty – I think he's lovely." I don't remember much else to be honest. He obviously did say things from the Bible, but I can't remember exactly what.' But she was touched by his prayers for their family.

The other thing that stuck in Lorna's mind was Roy saying, 'It's a serious thing getting your child baptised. A lot of people wouldn't allow you to because you aren't coming to church.' Lorna did go to church a few times – with her mum, never with Jason – but then stopped. Very few people spoke to her. She thinks that perhaps she looked as though she didn't want to be spoken to. Or perhaps the church had got used to baptism families turning up to services for a few weeks, never to be seen again once they had got what they wanted. Why bother getting to know them?

Lorna's experience of church might have been mixed, but the baptism service had a far bigger impact on her than the cynical churchgoers would have expected. Lorna knew that she had said she believed things that in fact she knew very little about. She had also promised to bring Bo up as a Christian and bring her to church. Over the next few years she felt bad that she had not kept her promises. Jason had made the same promises, but they had no effect on him.

Lorna, Jason and Bo were also added to the church prayer list. A faithful group would regularly pray for those families who had had children baptised. For most of the group, the families were just names on a list, but they prayed for these strangers for years. Could those prayers really make a difference?

CHAPTER 10

A second family event happened that knocked everything off course. Jason's younger brother, Kevin, had been using heroin for some time and his addiction had destroyed his health. When he should have been in his prime, in his early thirties, he had Aids, HIV and hepatitis A, B and C. The last straw was an attack by a drug dealer, who bit a chunk out of his face. He was clearly dying, drifting in and out of consciousness, when Jason visited him in hospital.

Once again Jason's sense of loyalty to his undeserving brother nearly got him into serious trouble. Jason tried to force his brother to give him the dealer's name, but Kevin refused. Jason planned to come back the next day to try again. By then Kevin was dead. 'For a good few years I was gutted. I would have gone and done the geezer. Again it was God at work. I would have killed him without a doubt – specially after my brother died.'

Jason had been thwarted in his desire to hurt the man responsible for his brother's death. At the funeral he was ready for a fight. Jason insulted another customer in the pub, where the wake was being held. 'If someone says something to you at a wake, you just take it and walk away normally. But this fella went and got some mates and come back.' Within a few minutes Jason and a friend had beaten up all five of the other gang, then disappeared before the police arrived. 'I remember thinking it was his own fault, he shouldn't have come back. I was looking for a fight really.'

Jason was still struggling after his brother's death when he went to a Butlin's holiday park with a big group of friends. He wasn't in the mood for a party, and had booked a single room where he planned to take the huge stash of drugs he had brought with him. 'Just after my brother died, we went to Butlin's in Bognor. There was about twenty-five of us went. I took ketamine and Charlie and MDMA. It was going to be a heavy weekend. I'm not in a good frame of mind, if I'm honest. I come back Friday night and was just taking massive amounts of drugs, all through to Saturday morning.' That amount of drugs was bound to affect him, but his previous experience of ketamine had been particularly bad. 'Ketamine is just mental. I took it once, when I was round my mate's house. It sends you to a different planet. When I come to, my mate's missus looked a bit scared and said, "Jason, you must never take that stuff again, you are mental."'

By Saturday evening Jason was experiencing feelings of paranoia, convinced that everyone was out to get him. His friends had to stop him attacking random people in a club. In a moment of clarity Jason decided to go back to his own room to keep himself and others safe. He was still very confused and ended up lost, in the staff quarters. When security turned up, his drug-fried brain saw them as assassins set on murdering him. There was nothing nearby that could be used as a weapon, so Jason ran through a door and up the stairs into the staff accommodation area. From then on things went from bad to worse. 'They come up the stairs following me. There's this big, square window. I just went and barged it with my elbow, broke the window and snapped off a big, long shard of glass, which stopped them in their tracks. I said, "If you come any further, I'm gonna cut the three of you. I'll stab you in the neck." They are sort of edging forward. "I'm telling ya, if you come near me, I'm gonna cut ya."'

The police were called to deal with a siege situation. In scenes familiar from TV dramas, they tried to negotiate with Jason over the phone. 'I was talking to them on the phone saying, "There's hit men and they've come to kill me." "No, they're bouncers." "No, they're hit men." I looked out the window and there's now police with the shields and the riot gear on – probably about twenty old bill, loads of motors. They was up on the opposite balcony as well. All trying to talk me down. They was saying, "Come out quietly. Put the glass down." I just kept breaking bits of the window and throwing it at them. Chucking it at the police, who were there with their shields just blocking it. I was saying, "How do I know you are the real police?" They put the lights on and the sirens to show that they were the real police so I would come out.'

Jason only knows what happened at that stage of the evening because he heard about it later when he was in the dock. He can't personally remember any of the events. Jason's behaviour clearly left a lasting impression on the others that were there, who then very graphically described the experience in court.

Back at Butlin's, Jason gradually came to and became more aware of his surroundings. 'People was coming out the rooms – I was like, "Get back in." They all ran back in terrified. They was all hostages really. It went on for an hour and a half or so. Then I started calming down a little bit. I realised who the police were. I said, "I'm coming down – you had better take me nicely or this is going to go off." So they said, "Yeah alright, Jason. Just come down. Put the glass down…" So I got down on my knees and put the glass down.' Police in riot gear charged through the door and wrestled Jason to the ground. Jason tried to fight back, but the policemen were protected by their helmets and visors, and soon had Jason in cuffs.

His first stop was an ambulance to be checked over. There was nothing physically wrong with him, but Jason was worried that he would get beaten up in the police van, so he invented various medical conditions that would keep him in the ambulance. He wanted his cuffs loosened. When the police officer refused, Jason responded in predictable Jason fashion. As his hands were cuffed, his head was his only weapon. 'Bam – so I nutted him coz he wouldn't loosen them. I'm just head butting and trying to bite. They are just punching me and weighing me in.

There was this poor guy trying to stop us and calm it all down.' Eventually they managed to calm him down again and loosened the cuffs.

Jason was then taken to hospital for further tests. It was obvious he had taken large quantities of drugs and his heart needed to be checked. As they stuck sticky pads on his chest to attach the heart monitor, he could hear the police talking about him to the medical staff. One of them was being less than complimentary. That set Jason off again. 'So bam, I nutted him. We started fighting again. The other two jumped on me and started weighing me in. The nurse and doctor are going, "Stop!" They calmed me down again. I ended up going on the monitor and then they got me down the station.'

Jason was still high, which made him not only dangerously violent but also, apparently, hysterically funny. 'Although I was mental and was fighting them, they said I was really funny. I had them in hysterics. My mind had just gone. I was in this world of ketamine and things. I'm mental enough as it is without taking that stuff.' And Jason wasn't just fighting the police. When he found out that the prisoner in front of him was accused of sexual assault, he tried to attack him too. Jason still had a sense of morality – of acceptable and unacceptable crimes.

He was treated extraordinarily leniently. 'The old bill were alright really. They said "You haven't been in trouble for ten years." That was what they thought. I hadn't been *caught* for ten years. It looked good on me. I went to court and got done for affray. To be honest, because

I have been such an idiot all my life, the prosecution have never done deals with me. They have always gone for the full whack. But this time, I think because I was funny apparently – I can't remember a lot of it – I said I was going to plead not guilty. Affray would be six months to ten years. I said I would plead guilty if they would drop the charge to a lesser one – up to six months or a fine. I knew I could do six months easy.' Jason also helped his case by volunteering to go to drug rehab. A friend had suggested this. Jason didn't think he had a problem, but knew that it would look good in court. 'It helped me coz the judge turned round and just accepted the charge of lesser affray and he gave me a six or eight hundred pound fine. He said I had to pay it by midday or I was going away for four months or something. So I paid it straight away.'

Jason could have been sent to prison for ten years, but got away with a relatively small fine. He was in his late thirties, with a wife and two daughters and running a successful business. He could have lost it all. Surely this was the time to turn over a new leaf and give up the violence, drink and drugs – or was it too late already?

CHAPTER 11

Lorna had been unimpressed by Jason's latest exploits. She had been at home with baby Bo. And although she knew what Jason could be like, what had happened at Butlin's had been extreme even for him. She longed for a stable family life and wanted to buy their own home. Jason wasn't bothered. 'We were living with Lorna's mum. Before that we were in a flat above the office, which was a dump really. I had no aspiration to buy my own house. I was from a council estate, so I just didn't think like that. As long as I had money in my pocket, I was happy.' Lorna got her way. Two years after Bo was born, they moved into their new home. Maybe this was the new start they needed.

A month before the move, Jason's much-loved mother was diagnosed with cancer. Seven months later, she died. Jason had previously said of his family, 'We don't care. If one of us died tomorrow, we'd probably say, "That's another one gone."' However, he had not coped well after his brother's death, even though he had never had a good relationship with him and his brother had caused him nothing but trouble. Grief had still hit him hard. He adored his mother. She had been the one loving presence in his childhood, and he had always tried to protect her. He couldn't do anything to protect her now, and he was devastated. 'She was diagnosed end of November, and was dead by the twentieth of June. It was quite rapid, and only a year and a half or two years after my brother had died – my little brother, Kevin. That was a tough time.'

Jason's reaction to Kevin's death had been to fight and consume industrial quantities of drugs. Initially his response to his mother's death was more positive. He ran the London Marathon to raise money for the hospice that had cared for her. He had actually signed up for the race while she was still alive. After she died, his running training gave him focus, but also just postponed his grief. 'It didn't hit me at first because I was busy working and I had decided to do the London Marathon for my mum – for the hospice. They had been really good to her. They give people the best they can give em. I was very impressed. They were very respectful. To the families who visit as well. My mum died and because I had started training for the marathon and signed up for it I did it in 2011.'

During the whole of the following year Jason didn't allow himself to grieve. He concentrated on work and on his training. For the final six months he was determined to get himself in shape, but things didn't go as planned.

'I started training quite a lot but kept getting blisters and shin splints. That held me back a lot. I was only really fit for ten miles.' He knew race day would be challenging, but in fact it started well. 'Off I went. I started running the race. I was doing OK. The first half of the marathon I did in three hours.' Halfway through the race Jason took a break in a Portaloo on the course. For twenty minutes he debated with himself whether he should carry on or not. 'But I had to finish. I had to do it. It was about fifteen miles in. I'm the kind of person who don't give up. I wasted twenty minutes in this toilet arguing with myself! I came back out and I finished it. It was hard. Really hard. The last half was about four hours because I twisted me knee, my knee was swollen, my feet were covered in blisters.' Jason had overcome the pain, honoured his mother's memory and raised money for the hospice. It might have been a different sort of fight, but once again Jason had fought and won.

Running a marathon was the kind of physical struggle Jason understood. He was used to experiencing pain and his working life consisted of hard manual labour. He was far less equipped to manage the heart-breaking emotional turmoil he felt when he finally had to confront the reality of the loss of his mother. Immediately after the marathon Jason's life began to spiral out of control. At the end of the garden Jason had earlier built his very own, fully stocked bar – somewhere to chill with friends or find some peace and quiet. Over the following months he spent more and more time there alone, beginning the night of the marathon. 'On the way home in the cab, I made a phone call and got some cocaine dropped off. There was a back alleyway to the bar at the end of the garden, so not even Lorna knew. They used to slip it under the door, so no one ever knew. I got on it that night and I remember "Bang", the grief of my mum hit me. That was hard. I was all confused and off me face. I walked up to the house and lay down. I couldn't move for three days coz my legs were just ruined. I went to go up the stairs and I couldn't even lift my legs to go up.'

This was far more than post-race exhaustion. Jason entered a very dark place. He was drinking and taking drugs, but this time all on his own. 'The grief had hit me then. I was just getting sadder and sadder. I started drinking more, taking drugs more. And I stopped going out. I used to be really sociable. I was the one who everyone would know was there if I was in the pub. I had violent feelings. I'd look at people and I'd just think, "I'm gonna kill him." I knew I was dangerous at that time. So I kept myself in. I just went into myself in my bar at the bottom of my garden. I had to go to work – I hated it. I didn't want to be around people. Over the course of a few years, I was going further and further downhill.'

Lorna was aware that Jason was hurting, but there wasn't much she could do to help. She just helplessly watched on as their marriage suffered. 'After his mum's death was the hardest time. Hard, dark times. He was short-tempered. He had no patience and didn't like me doing things. I couldn't just go out when I wanted to or say I'm popping into my sister's. I don't know if it was him feeling not safe? But weekends he would just be drinking. He'd just be in the living room with the curtains closed really. We were getting further and further apart. The worst times were when Bo was at school – not straight after his mum died – from when she was four or five. He was never really nasty to me; he never hit me. I did feel alone sometimes. If we had a row, he could get quite angry, but he wouldn't hit me – he'd hit a door or something. I wouldn't say I was frightened of him. Bo has never been frightened of him. We weren't doing anything together, that's the thing.'

Lorna had been very close to Jason's mum as well, but grief drove her and Jason apart rather than together. 'When his mum went, he lost his rock. She had always been there and knew him. In a way that's what she became for me as well – she knew what a violent partner is like. Although Jason wasn't violent to the extent of his dad – he's never hit me or his kids; I never had to run away from him – she understood.' They both missed her. 'We didn't talk about it together, though.'

Jason's life was at its lowest ebb. His marriage was in trouble, he had cut himself off from his friends, he was depressed, and his drug and alcohol consumption were out of control. All his life Jason had used violence to respond to threats. Violence was of no use now. He had got through other situations with self-discipline and sheer hard work. Neither could help him cope with the darkness of grief he experienced after his mother's death.

From early childhood he had taken care of himself and, against the odds, he had survived, but nothing in his armoury could handle this emotional trauma. Jason was at rock bottom. Could things get any worse?

CHAPTER 12

None of Jason's normal strategies were working. Rather than lifting, Jason's grief was growing deeper and darker. Maybe he needed to look for a different kind of help – help from a greater power than himself. It was a good instinct, but Jason made a disastrous wrong turn. He had never believed in the supernatural, but if there was a chance that he could get in touch with his mum, he was ready to try anything. 'I'm drinking more and more and felt in a dark, dark place. I remember people at work talking about how they had seen ghosts. I've never seen a ghost or anything like that in my life – nothing. I watched these ghost programmes and horror films, and thought, "What a load of rubbish" – all of it. God as well. But then – when I was down in the bar on my own, in the dark, watching a bit of telly, sniffing and drinking, coz I was missing my mum so much – I thought I would give it a go. I started dabbling in these things of contacting the dead and all that.' In desperation Jason downloaded a Ouija board app on to his phone. 'I didn't believe for a second that anything would happen.' At first nothing did.

When strange things did start to happen, Jason tried to explain them away. He had seen things before when he had been on drugs – maybe this was just another bad trip. 'It took a while, maybe six to eight months, and little things started happening. I just felt there was a presence around – not a very nice presence. I thought, "This is just the drugs. I'm paranoid." And then I would hear little things and see little things. I remember there was a toilet in the back of the bar, and I went out there once and I see this black figure go under the garage door. I just looked. I thought I must be tripping or something, but I knew it was real. I convinced myself it wasn't, then I would hear these bangs and crashes. Weird things. The dog would go mental outside the bar.' Jason knew what was happening was different from his drug-fuelled experiences.

Lorna saw the dog's strange behaviour and was frightened. 'There was one time he was down the bar and I'm stuck in the house on my own, and the dog was just going mad – and he was quite a placid dog. He's running out to the kitchen, out to the living room, looking up the stairs. It was freaking me out. I don't usually worry – I'd rather just keep things in and not talk about them – and I don't even get overexcited about stuff. That annoys Jason sometimes. But this day the dog was scaring me because he kept looking up the stairs. I've never felt scared before. I phoned Jason up and then I phoned my sister up because I had never seen the dog acting like that before. They say dogs can sense things. I didn't know that Jason was looking into that app thing.'

You might have expected Jason to stop using the Ouija board app. In fact, he used it more and more. He still wasn't sure if it was real, but if it possibly was, there was still a chance he could contact his mother. 'Things were getting heavier – not just things happening around me, but mentally as well. I was still dabbling and trying to contact my mum on these apps and other ways. I don't know what I thought really. Somehow it had some sort of control over my mind to keep me wanting to find out more. It was enticing me to do it more. So I was doing it more. I was ignoring the danger signs because I didn't really think it was true.'

The weird and terrifying experiences continued – lights flickering, strange apparitions, banging doors. Understandably Jason was still not convinced that he wasn't having a breakdown or just reaping the consequences of decades of drug abuse. He was convinced that he was in trouble and needed help. He knew that this was not a problem that he could fix himself. Finally Jason looked to the only one actually able to improve his situation. In desperation, and with little expectation of an answer, Jason prayed. 'I remember when I was doing all this and went into the dark place, that's when I first called on God, which is a significant bit. I can't remember exactly when it was, but I was crying in my hands one night, when I was in the bar. I couldn't smile anymore. I didn't want to smile. I was so down. I was in such a dark place, and I was just ratty and horrible. I just said, "God, if there is a God, please help me. Just help me." Only looking back can I see that that is when things first started to change.'

Very shortly afterwards Jason told Lorna he had a problem. Lorna was pleased that he had opened up to her and was asking for help. She thought Jason's problem could be sorted by a doctor, probably a psychiatrist. 'She said I had to go to the doctors and speak to them – which I did. I told them, but things didn't really change. It was still getting worse on this spiritual side. At least I had started to know I had a problem. This was new. I couldn't work this out. I couldn't get my head round this really.'

One weekend, when he was home on his own, Jason experienced a whole range of inexplicable manifestations. He still wondered whether he was hallucinating, tripping or having a mental health crisis. 'It was getting progressively worse. Lorna went on a weekend away with the girls to Spain. Bo went to Kellie's. I was left at home alone. They went on the Saturday morning. Saturday afternoon I was smoking a fag out the back and I see this figure up at the window – black and white. I couldn't really make it out. Scraggy hair, with like a white nightie / dress-type thing on, just sitting at the window. Just looking at me. Every time I went for a fag it was there. It hadn't moved. And then I see two blokes, or they looked like blokes. It was a weird vision thing. They didn't look very nice. I just thought, "What's happening to me? Am I losing the plot?" I just sensed it. I went to bed.'

That night brought further strange happenings. 'I remember waking up at about two in the morning. It's pitch black, but I could see figures around me. I thought I must be dreaming and went back to sleep. I woke up at about seven in the morning and I had the sheet over my head because the light was coming in through the window. Through the sheet I could see these little black figures darting about. I pulled the cover off and there was nothing there. I could hear all these voices, but I couldn't make out what they were saying. I felt scratches going down my legs. I looked and I had little scratch marks all down my legs – little claw marks. I thought, "Am I doing this to myself?" I put my fingers down – and it didn't match my fingers. I thought I was having a breakdown or something.

'I was lying there and could hear all these noises downstairs. I went downstairs. The dog is terrified. He wouldn't move, he was so scared. I went in the front room and the light is swinging left to right. The voices stopped as soon as I went in the front room. Then I could hear the voices upstairs in the bedroom. I stopped the light swinging. Then I heard the cupboard door go "bang". I'd run out there and all the cupboard doors would be open. "What is happening?" Then there would be another bang in the front room again, like it was tormenting me. So I ran in there. I was all ready to fight, shouting and all that. I've heard all this commotion upstairs and run upstairs.

I had my video camera on, and I could see these figures through the video camera, but I can't see them with my own eyes. So I was using the camera to try and kick at them. I didn't video it, I was just looking through it. The dog was outside and just wouldn't come into the house. He was terrified. I thought maybe this is real then. Maybe something is happening. The realisation that this could be real was starting to come on me. I was scared.'

Lorna was scared too after she phoned Jason from Spain. 'While I was away, I called him, and he just said that some things had been happening. Kellie was bringing Bo back that night and it scared me. To be honest, what I thought was that he had been on drugs. I was scared for Bo to come back because I'm thinking what state is he in? He didn't normally take em if he knew he was having Bo – he would be clean. I knew he would look after her. But it did scare me because he was saying, "I've had enough."'

Jason was worried about Bo coming back to the house too. Kellie was bringing her back at five on Sunday afternoon. At four Jason ended up praying again. 'It got to about four and I knew Bo was due back soon. I tried to speak to my mum. "Mum, if you can hear me, stop all this going on." That threw me onto God. I said, "Dear God, I don't know what I've done. I need help. Please help me."' He had a few minutes' peace before he heard a loud bang from upstairs and felt the whole house shake. He ran to the bedroom but, as expected, there was no one there. Then it was over – for now.

But Jason was still terrified. He now knew that he was not just imagining things – he had the scratches to prove it. He was in a fight with an invisible enemy. A fight which, for the first time, he didn't think he could win. 'I was scared. I was worried for my family. I thought, "What have I done?" The realisation of it all hit me. The previous eighteen months had been building up to this weekend. I've done all sorts of drugs. I've done tripping before and all sorts of things, and I know the difference between that and reality. This was real. I knew I had to protect my family. I knew deep inside that I'd put my family in danger. I'd done that little prayer to God. Things calmed down.'

Jason was still on edge when Bo came home. Bo was about seven at the time. 'Kellie brought Bo home. She said, "You alright?" "Yeah, everything's fine." Inside I'm in pieces. I'm trying to act brave. It was now about nine o'clock and I took Bo into bed with me. I wanted to protect her. We were laying in bed together, but I wasn't going to sleep. I'm gonna protect my baby. Bo turned round and said, "What did you say that for, Dad? I'm not allowed to say that word." "What word? Spell it."' When Bo spelt it out, Jason was shocked. 'Something had said that word to Bo. That was when I really thought, "What have I done?" I have brought my family into danger.'

Lorna had commented on the dog's strange behaviour before, but this was the first time whatever was harassing Jason had interacted with any of his family directly. Throughout his life Jason had been committed to protecting the women and children in his life. The thought that their safety was threatened, and he could do nothing to help, was unbearable. He had always been able to dispatch threats with a few well-aimed punches, but this was different. He didn't know what he was up against. He couldn't see what he was up against. He did know he was losing the fight.

CHAPTER 13

When Jason had prayed, things had improved. He still wasn't sure about God, but he was desperate. None of his friends or family were Christians, so he went to the only religious place he knew. 'That's when I decided I had to get God involved. I thought of St Lawrence straight away, coz I got married there.' Jason didn't know that the vicar that had married them and baptised Bo had recently retired. He did know that the vicar lived in the house behind the church, so that is where he headed, though he kept changing his mind. 'As I was driving to the church, I just thought, I'll just go to work. The next thing I know, I'm knocking at David's door. All of a sudden, I was there. That bit in between I can't remember!' Jason hadn't expected to be at David's door. David certainly hadn't expected to see Jason there. 'So I come and knock on David's door. I think David was a bit taken aback, this big skinhead on his doorstep. I was crying. I had tears in my eyes, coz I knew I'd mucked up.'

Most people would think Jason had 'mucked up' his whole life – violence, prison, drugs, drink. But Jason had thought that his life was normal. He was not as violent as many of his friends, and he had never been addicted to heroin. He had been in prison a couple of times – hadn't everyone? He had avoided guns, and even knives most of the time. He had always stood up for those weaker and more vulnerable than him, and he was unswervingly loyal to those he loved.

There had been plenty of opportunities to change direction in his life so far. There had been good intentions and lucky escapes that had led nowhere. Prison, serious injury, Lorna's influence and the birth of his children had not been enough to turn his life around. Several times he had wanted to change, but his habits were too ingrained. It was just too hard. He was facing his toughest challenge yet and knew he could do nothing to help himself. Would the God, who he had had so little time for, really be able, or willing, to help him – if God existed at all?

David, slightly nervously, invited him in. Whether the things Jason was experiencing were caused by drugs, poor mental health or something more supernatural, David knew God was the only one who could help. Jesus had come to earth to rescue people who have mucked up.

'He brought me in, and he was telling me about Jesus. It was different to how we all were taught at school. You get the basics of it, but not the full power of Jesus – his majesty and grace and all the rest of it. If you think you're not good enough, that's it – you're not good enough.

Then you realise, actually he can save me and my family. That's how it was put to me. David obviously did a good job because I was totally hooked from that second. I was ready. I remember David saying to me, "Would you like me to pray with you to become a Christian?" I said, "Yeah." He prayed. I was in tears.'

David gave him a copy of Luke's Gospel to read and asked him to come back in a few days. 'He said come back on Friday. I don't know how David felt about it. He probably thought I weren't coming back.' David certainly thought it was unlikely he would see Jason again. But he did. Jason came back on the Friday, having read Luke's Gospel. He said he would come to church on Sunday with Lorna and Bo. David prayed but doubted that they would come. They did.

Jason had just made a unilateral decision that his family would now be attending church regularly. Lorna was shocked but pleased. She had suggested that they should go together a couple of years earlier. Bo had asked whether she was baptised. When she learnt that she was, she wanted to know why they didn't go to church. Lorna remembered the promises she had made at Bo's baptism and suggested that they go as a family. Jason had refused, and Lorna didn't want to go on her own. When Jason told her his plan to go to church, she was ready. 'I couldn't believe it. I never thought he would be someone who would be coming to church every Sunday. I was happy. Me and Bo were really up for coming. It is like God was at work in me and Bo first, helping us to be ready. Jason just needed that extra kick. I was really glad actually because I've always wanted to come to church to be honest.'

Lorna's grandmother had been to church when she was younger. She would read Lorna Bible stories and talk to Lorna about her faith. Tragically Lorna's younger brother died when he was seven and Lorna was twelve, leaving Lorna's mum angry and hurt. Lorna remembers her nan urging her mum not to give up on God. 'I wanted to know more, but I didn't really know how to do that. None of my friends went to church. I didn't think I would fit in. To be honest, I just used to think it was full of posh people! Not people that would want me there really.'

Jason felt the same, but was pleasantly surprised when he went to church for the first time. 'I felt very intimidated at first because I thought it was all full of posh people – people who might judge me. But it wasn't. It was full of people who were really kind, very welcoming, chatty. They believed what I believed, and some of them were really helpful in giving me direction and encouraging me to keep walking with Jesus.' Among the people who were particularly pleased to see Jason were Roy, who had visited their home for baptism preparation, and Andrew and Sue, who had been faithfully praying for the Armstrong family – just names on a list – for the past six years.

Until now Jason's knowledge of Christianity had consisted of black-and-white Bible epics on TV, mucking about as a youngster in the homes of very patient Christians (as he sheltered from the cold), and the occasional christening and wedding, including his own, when his mind was already on the party after. Like most people he knew that Christianity had something to do with going to church. Gradually, with the help of David and others at St Lawrence, Jason came to understand that there was much more to it than that. He understood that God loved him and welcomed him into his family, not because Jason deserved it – he definitely knew he didn't – but because of Jesus. When Jesus died on the cross, he had willingly taken on himself the punishment Jason – and all of us – deserve for turning our backs on God. By trusting in Jesus' death on his behalf, Jason was forgiven and given a new life with God in return.

It was a lot to take in. Jason had a lot to learn. 'I just wanted to know more. I thought, "If I am giving my life to this Jesus, I want to know I'm right." That day when I gave my life to Jesus, I meant it. I can't explain it to you – how that happened and why I was so ready – but I was ready. I just felt I've got to give it a go – this seems right to me. The more I was looking into it, the more I knew it was right.' Jason met up with David regularly to read the Bible together and pray. He was also finding Christian content on YouTube to help answer some of his many questions.

Jason looked back on the life he had lived – a life so different from the perfect life he saw Jesus living as he read Luke's Gospel. He knew Jesus had paid for his sin and that he was forgiven, but he also knew he had to face up to the things he had done if he was going to turn his back on his old way of life and follow Jesus' way instead. 'The gravity of my sin, that I'd put my family in danger, how I'd been

as a husband, dad – the weight of all that come upon me.
You've got the weight of my sin and the realisation of
all the bad things I'd been doing. We all like to think we
are alright people, and the things I done in the past were
because they deserved it in my eyes, or they had it coming,
whatever. You justify things like that. There is no hiding
when you become a Christian. You have to face up to
these sinful ways, these sinful desires. It was tough. Every
day I'm saying sorry for a different thing that's coming to
my mind – someone I had really hurt or beat up, people
I've cut. It's terrible. I didn't use to lose any sleep over
any of them, but now every one of them is hurting me.
Every day I'm going through that. I'd remember some
bad thoughts I had about killing someone, even to think
em is bad enough. I spent a lot of time saying sorry and
asking for forgiveness.'

Jason had to confront his past, but he also needed to
know that God had forgiven him for every part of it.
'I remember one day I was having a fag one morning out
by the back door, and I remember thinking to myself,
"I don't feel guilty anymore." The guilt had gone. It makes
me very emotional that. I thought, "Thank you, Lord."'
When someone turns their life over to God, God also
promises them peace because his Holy Spirit comes to live
with them. Jason experienced a calm he had never known
before. 'Things did start to change. I had a calmness come
over me that I can't explain.'

Jason thought the disturbing demonic visions and
attacks were his biggest issue, and he knew that his drug

habit was getting very expensive. God knew that they were not his most serious problems. Jason needed God if he was going to live life as it had been designed to be lived – the kind of life that helped rather than hurt people, that loved rather than hated; the kind of life that lasted beyond death to enjoy life in God's perfect place forever. For that he needed forgiveness and a new life. That is what God gave him.

CHAPTER 14

The family was going to church each Sunday and Bo was enjoying Sunday Club. David was meeting with Jason each week. Lorna started meeting up with someone to read the Bible too. Jason's transformation was dramatic. Lorna's was less obvious, but just as profound. 'I've always believed in God. I always had a Bible growing up. I used to have a picture one and then I had this other one. Was it a Gideon or something? I always used to look through it, but I liked the visual things – so Adam and Eve and Noah and the Easter story. I didn't really know the Bible. I just took bits out that I understood – bits I thought I understood. I hadn't really thought about what Jesus had done for me until we started coming as a family. Then it was WOW.' Jason wasn't sure that Lorna was a Christian. He needn't have worried. 'I just keep things very low-key. Perhaps he didn't realise what was going on.'

For the previous few years, the family had been falling apart. When he wasn't working, Jason spent most of his time in the bar at the end of the garden or in the living room with the curtains closed. He was short-tempered and controlling. Jason was cutting himself off from Lorna and Bo but was jealous of their close relationship. Now the family began to heal. 'As a family we were going to church and things were getting better. One of the first things I noticed was that one day we was having a laugh. It was probably about a year in. We had been out somewhere – I had just used to stay in all the time. Since my mum died, it had been years since there had been laughter like that in the house. I thought, "Thank you, Lord." He's saved this family. He's helping us. Things were starting to change.'

Lorna noticed it too. 'Doing things together is the main thing. We feel just really happy. Life isn't any better as in work and things like that. We still have our ups and downs with work, and he still gets on my nerves sometimes! But when you know you are loved by Jesus that much, then you have got to forgive and love the things that other people do to you. That's what we have learnt as a family. We are going to get on each other's nerves as a family, but we've got to forgive. And it's not worth going on about it for a few days. Big changes!'

Jason the hard man was changing on the inside. Part of the new life God gives is a new, softer heart and Jason experienced emotions that he had never known before. Reading the Bible touched him deeply. 'It was a very emotional time as well. Sometimes I would be reading Luke's Gospel and feel all choked up.' Jason had always loved Lorna but hadn't known how to express it. 'I loved her but didn't know how to love. It's only since I become a Christian that I've learnt how to love properly and sincerely – not for selfish reasons, but for love itself. You know I couldn't show love. My thing with showing love is protecting someone. Like, I'd die for you. I've never actually been able to show love – until now, I mean. I've definitely changed – more loving. I mean now I can watch a sad movie and I'll have a tear in my eye. I've never done that before, and that's God. He opens up these new things. You feel more. You care more. I look at the world now and I feel for it.'

Jason could see the difference God was making in his life, but was frustrated that he couldn't change more quickly. 'I'm slowly starting to change. There's just little signs that I'm changing into a different person. I'm getting more patient, less angry, more forgiving. Only little bits at a time. I wanted to do more. I was committed to Jesus.'

Lorna is convinced that the changes that Jesus was making in Jason's life saved their relationship. She also saw the impact on Jason's relationship with his friends. Lorna had always been quiet and sensible, and as a woman, perhaps it was more acceptable that she was interested in Christianity. But Jason's friends found his new faith incomprehensible. 'They were shocked that we had started coming to church. When we was out with my uncle Paul and his partner one time, he said to Jason, "Oh well, she's always been into that sort of thing." Jason feels that he has lost a lot of friends. He feels quite lonely. He says, "I don't feel like I've got any friends at all." It's like there was something different about both of us.'

Lorna had always been happy with a small group of good friends, and before Jason's self-imposed isolation of the previous months, she'd stayed at home with Bo while Jason was out drinking and taking drugs with his mates. 'I've never been popular, but I've never wanted to be. But he wanted to be. I was quite happy to sit there quiet with no one talking to me. He'd have to be at the heart of it. It's been harder for him because he's lost that. But I said, "Were they your real friends? If they are not with you now, they were with you because you were loud, because you used to buy them drinks or whatever else you gave them."'

Jason was learning that living as a Christian did not mean living an easier life. Losing 'friends' was only one of the challenges he faced. As life became more difficult, would his new faith survive?

CHAPTER 15

When Jason was at his most desperate, under attack from supernatural forces, he had prayed. The banging doors, flashing lights and shadowy figures had tormented him less often. Now that he was a Christian, he hoped they would leave him alone. He also knew that cocaine could not be a part of his new life, and he assumed that God would take away his addiction. He was frustrated by how slowly his character was being transformed. He was even more frustrated by his inability to kick his drug habit. And the malevolent forces in his home continued to plague him and the family. Was it all worth it? Could God really change the habits of a middle-aged man who had known nothing but violence, addiction and crime his entire life?

In the past, when Jason had set out to achieve something, he had often succeeded. His injured arm had healed beyond the doctor's expectations because he had done his exercises diligently, despite the pain. He had finished the London Marathon even though he ran the last miles in agony. He had built up the family building firm by putting in long hours of manual labour – and by persevering after the 2008 financial crisis almost saw the business collapse. Surely God would honour the same sort of hard work and reward him by taking away the drugs and demons? He couldn't understand why that wasn't happening. He was doing everything a 'good Christian' should do – wasn't he? 'I was praying to take these drugs away. I'm going, "Please let it stop." I was getting very frustrated. I'm going to church every week. I'm committed. I'm going to all the courses, Christianity Explored, the prayer meetings, on the church council. I'm doing everything. I'm just thinking, "God, where are you? Where are you? Why are you letting me do this, God? Why are you forsaking me?" I was getting so angry.'

Jason was fighting a secret battle. He had told David initially about his drug use, but hadn't let on how severe the addiction was. He had cut down how much and how often he was taking cocaine – 'I'd got it down to once every two and a half to three weeks. Instead of doing five, six, seven, eight grammes in an evening, I was doing one or two.' However, he was unable to stop completely. He also realised that the weird happenings in his house seemed to coincide with his relapses.

'It was getting bad as a Christian because I'm feeling really deserted by God in some ways. I'm thinking, "Is he still there? Is he really there?" I'm getting angrier with God, I noticed at that time. Changes had been happening in my life. It's two years I've been a Christian now, but this battle is still going on and it's a tough one. I was thinking I was doing a great job at being dedicated as a Christian. I'd read my Bible and pray. I was reading up on stuff and watching YouTube videos from good Christian people to learn more about my faith, trying to gain more strength, trying to be a better person as well. But I think I was getting weaker and weaker at that time, if I'm honest. It's just getting tougher and tougher. Spiritually I'm really being tested. This demonic stuff is still happening. I'm still relapsing every two and a half to three weeks, which was tough because I was a Christian. To be taking drugs and letting God down as a Christian is hard. I knew I shouldn't be doing it. I knew God was not happy with me doing it. Yet I still done it. With addiction, the moment you wake up till the moment you go to sleep your brain is going, "Get drugs, get drugs, get drugs…" All day long. You can be talking to someone, but in your mind all you are thinking about is getting drugs. The other part of me – the Holy Spirit – is going, "NO." I had had enough. It's got to stop. "How long, Lord?" This row is going on between me and God. Why is he letting me go through all this suffering?'

The problem was that Jason was still trying to fight his own battles. Even though he thought he was 'letting God down' by taking drugs, the solution he expected was for God to remove his addiction. Jason had thought this was how God would 'reward' him for all his Christian activities. But there was only one thing that God wanted him to do, as Jason himself knew. 'During all this time I had a voice in my head saying, "Tell David. Tell David."

I couldn't tell David because I thought I had let him down. The more I got angry with God, the more this voice was telling me to tell David. I just can't face David. I can't tell him. This is all getting more intense. It's this battle. I tell myself it is all in my head. I think it was God talking to me, I really do.'

While this battle for Jason's will was raging, he was losing his battle with drugs. Over the past months Jason had been reducing his intake, but now, over just a few days, all this progress was reversed. Willpower alone was not enough for Jason to overcome his drug addiction. 'I relapsed three days in a row, and that hadn't happened in all the time I've been fighting it. I'm convinced it was the devil at work. I would be at the traffic lights, and the dealer I hadn't seen for ages would be there and go, "Jay, I've got something here for you. Try that." Three times in a row that happened. It had never happened before in my life. Weird! It was crazy. After relapsing three times, I know I've got to tell David.'

At the same time, the strange happenings were still going on at home – something else that Jason was reluctant to share at church. 'It was getting more intense and they was doing more things that Lorna and Bo had seen. They were changing tack a bit and I didn't like it. One night they were pulling the dog around again, mucking about and things. I was in bed, looking at my phone, and something snatched my phone out of my hand. So I've jumped out the bed to confront this thing that was standing there, and I smashed my head. It was like it was made of steel. It hurt so bad. Something was there and then it was gone. That freaked me out a little bit. A few nights later I was about to go to sleep, just about to drop off, and I see this dark figure out my eye. It jumped at me on the bed. It was so heavy and strong. I couldn't even move an inch. It was strangling me and I couldn't breathe. I was trying to fight with all my might, but I couldn't move – not even a millimetre, I was so pinned down. I've got my eyes wide open and I'm looking at Lorna, but I couldn't talk or anything and I'm going blue. I just prayed to God. I said, "Lord, help me." Bang. Gone. Just like that. It dissipated. It was finished. I jumped up, gasping for air. I was terrified. Luckily enough Lorna stayed asleep. I didn't wake her or tell her about it.'

Jason was quite used to these experiences – they were becoming part of his everyday life – but he still couldn't explain them to himself, let alone other people. Was he imagining it? Was it the drugs? 'I kept getting scratched. I did show the claw marks to a couple of people. They just think you did it yourself. I used to think, "Did I do it myself?" I got strangled a couple of times. Scratched over a hundred times. Things thrown at me many a time. Doors slamming. Knocking at the door and no one there. All these kind of things. They torment you. I see these figures as well. I remember once, when I was laying in bed, Bo was in bed with us. I woke up about four or five in the morning. I see this big, tall, black, thin figure pulling Bo down the bed. I've jumped up and turned the light on. It just walked out the door. Gone. I pulled Bo back up into the bed. I'm just awake. I just can't sleep – I didn't sleep much during that time, I was always trying to protect my family.'

If it had just been Jason who saw things, the drugs would have been a simple explanation, but increasingly Lorna saw things too. She saw the scratches mysteriously appear on Jason's legs several times. 'We was sitting on the sofa and it happened. You could just see it appearing redder as he was just sitting there. I used to think that these were just things in films. Now I know there is a spiritual world and he opened up something.' She heard the doors slamming, the rhythmic knocking in the middle of the night, and saw the lights throughout the house flickering and swinging. 'It even happened when my mum was there, and she goes, "Oh these lights." I said, "I know. It's really scaring me." She says, "It's probably just the wiring!"' But the wiring had just been redone, so Lorna knew that wasn't the problem. She tried to push it all to the back of her mind. 'I think I was scared to think about it in case it fuelled them. So I didn't like talking about it. If people started talking about it to me, I didn't want to.'

Bo was having nightmares, which was unlike her. Jason and Lorna generally managed to protect her from all the strange happenings inside their home. 'All that stuff, if you asked her now, she wouldn't know a thing about it because we hid it well. We would say, "It was the wind – or this or that."' But this wasn't always easy to do. Lorna only once saw one of the dark figures that tormented

Jason, but so did Bo. 'Me and Bo was on the couch once, just watching telly. It faces the wall and the door to our lounge is next to it. I thought I saw like this black head sort of come round. But you know when your eyes play tricks, and I thought, "Oh, I'm just seeing things." Then Bo said she'd seen it and she got really scared and was crying. I'm trying to play it down for her sake, saying it's just your eyes are playing tricks, but I had seen it as well at the same time.'

Jason was sleep deprived, fighting addiction and dealing with the guilt that came from knowing that his actions had led to his family living through a real-life horror movie. But he was still convinced that, given the right tools and techniques, he was brave and tough enough to take his tormentors on. 'I remember once, when all this demonic stuff was getting too much, I'd come home one day and it started again. I couldn't stop it this time after I took the drugs. The lights started and the noises started again. The dog would come running into the front room sometimes and you'd see him being pulled back while he's still trying to run forward. I'd go, "Leave him alone" and run at him. Then they'd let him go. He'd come up terrified. The things I put that dog through! I feel terrible. I thought, "That's it, I'm gonna fight em and let em have it." So I rung David up and said, "Get me some holy water." I was going to do em once and for all. I was planning to tape some knives to my hands, throw holy water on em and call it on! Just have it to the death. That's my nature – to fight. I never had no fear of nothing. I wasn't frightened of death.

I didn't care. You are a dangerous man if you don't care if you live or die.

'David said, "Come and see me at four o'clock." I came to see him. I was ready for a fight. He just calmed me down. He said, "Don't call them on or anything like that. That's very, very dangerous. You can't do that. Walk with Jesus. Trust in Jesus."' Jason was trusting in Jesus, but he was also trusting in his own ability to fight any threat to his family's safety. Trusting did not come easily, and looking to someone else, even God himself, to fight his battles for him went against every instinct.

If anything, these demonic events had got darker and more dangerous since Jason became a Christian. Was it a sign that God's enemy wasn't going to give up his prey without a fight? 'Not long after that on the Saturday morning, about ten o'clock in the morning, I was in bed and I could smell this disgusting smell like drains, sewers, even worse than that. Then I see this black figure just coming out the wall – huge, about nine and a half feet tall. It was hunched over our ceiling. I couldn't see any features. It was the blackest black you could ever imagine. I knew it weren't human because its hands weren't human. It was coming towards me slowly – really slowly. I'm just looking, thinking, "What's going on here?" As it's come, it's knelt on the bed. It was so big the whole bed went craaackkk. I just prayed to God. It was the first time ever I thought I was going to be killed. I had this really intense feeling this thing was going to kill me. I just prayed to God and, all of a sudden, this light just appeared. The only way I can explain it was like a big uncut diamond – all jaggedly shaped, with bits coming out. Pure white light. It just went "Boof!" on this thing. I'm just laying there watching this, thinking, "What is going on?" I was mesmerised by it. The thing is trying to push against the light and the light is pushing it back. It just dissipated. All gone. The smell had gone – everything. It must have been God or an angel…' However tough he was, Jason realised that he was powerless against these dark forces. Only God could defeat them. Trusting in Jesus and walking with Jesus really was the only way.

Jason had to learn the same lesson with his drug addiction. Willpower, good intentions and trying to be a 'good' Christian were never going to break the grip that cocaine had on his life. Trusting in Jesus and walking with Jesus was the only way. He had resisted telling David for so long. He now believed that finally confessing his drug habit was the one action needed for God to set him free from it. 'I'd relapsed really bad that week and I thought I've got to tell him. This Sunday I'm going to tell David. I come to church psyched up that I'm going to do this.' When Sunday came, Jason discovered that David was preaching in another church. 'My world just fell apart. I thought, "NO! NO!" Finally I've plucked up the courage to do it.'

Determined to tell someone while he had the nerve, Jason instead confided in Martin, the assistant minister, and asked him to tell David. Later that week Jason finally met up with David and explained the situation. 'I didn't tell him it all, but I did tell him I'd been relapsing and struggled with drugs. We had a good chat and prayed together. I thought, "That's it. I've told David now. I've done what you've asked, Lord. This is it." Jason was convinced that now his need for drugs would miraculously vanish.

But the very next day he relapsed once again. Here was another fight that Jason had to admit he could not win by himself. He – wrongly – felt a complete failure as a Christian, and as a man. 'I honestly had no more fight in me. I fell to my knees that day. I remember it clear as day. I fell to my knees in tears and went, "You know what, I can't do this no more. I'm done. I give up." I could not fight anymore. I've tried as hard as I can try. I had given it my all. I had tried so hard to stop every time I relapsed. I tried everything. I'm fighting this all day, every day. I was more than devastated. It was worse than that. I can't even think of a word. It was a catastrophe. I was finished. I didn't have no fight left in me. I was done with it. I thought, "That's it. I'm going to die. Just leave em to it." I had thought of committing suicide and ending it all when I was down in the bar a few times. I was very close to it at one point. I fell to my knees that day, just crying, and said, "I've done everything you have asked of me, Lord. I've tried my best. I cannot fight no more." I was done. Literally done.'

Jason had been trying to bargain with God. He reckoned that if he did what God wanted – tell David about his drug addiction – then God would do what he wanted – take away his craving. He was learning that he couldn't bargain with God. Jason had thought that if he tried really hard, God would just provide the little bit of extra willpower he needed to break his habit. After all, Jason was used to fighting his own battles. But he now understood that he had to allow God to fight his battles for him. The only way to be victorious was by trusting in and walking with Jesus. It was a hard and humbling thing to realise, particularly for someone who had learnt from his childhood that no one else would look out for him and that to survive he had to fight.

God had brought Jason to his knees. If he was ever going to really trust and walk with Jesus, Jason needed to understand his own weakness and God's extraordinary power and love. Jason might have been the tough guy on the estate who could dispatch any threat with a few well-aimed punches, but God had allowed him to see how weak he really was. He had been unable to turn his life around despite good intentions, Lorna's love for him and the salutary deaths of good friends. Lifelong habits, his background and his environment made change impossible. Lifelong habits, his background and his environment meant that he didn't see change as essential or even particularly desirable. When he was faced with his addiction and supernatural evil, Jason was helpless, scared and out of his depth. He needed help, and only God had the power to help him. Finally Jason was able to acknowledge that walking with Jesus wasn't a bargain where he tried to live a 'good' Christian life in return for rewards from God. Trusting and walking with Jesus meant handing over everything to him, admitting his own weakness. Jason couldn't bargain with God; he just had to gratefully accept God's help as a loving gift.

From that moment Jason's craving for drugs was gone. It had taken a long time. 'From coming a Christian until the Lord took it away was about two years seven months.' Initially he was cautious. He knew that he had relapsed many times in the past – would this time really be different? A year later, he asked David, Martin – the assistant minster – and their wives out for a celebratory meal. He was now confident that God had removed the addiction for good. Having realised his own weakness, Jason could really appreciate God's strength.

CHAPTER 16

Many at church were completely unaware of Jason's struggles. They knew him as a loyal, helpful and generous friend and a committed member of the church. He and his family were at every service and midweek group – always willing to help out in whatever way was needed. And now this hard work was no longer used by Jason as a bargaining chip or an attempt to get into God's good books, but was a grateful response to all that God had done in his life. He knew that he could trust Jesus with everything, and wanted to walk with him in the life that God had created him to live. 'I gave myself to the Lord fully.'

Jason is very clear that being a Christian is not just about going to church on a Sunday. It means you want to 'get out there and graft for the Lord. Just do whatever he wants you to do. I cut grass and sort out the buildings and things – that's my little thing. I try and do it well. It matters to me that people see a church that's loved, and hopefully it makes them come in. You get loads of comments from people walking past if the graveyard looks nice. It's nice to hear because we put effort into it to make it happen and make it a welcoming church that's loved and looked after.' Jason does far more than that. As District Warden, he is a much-trusted member of the church leadership team. So as well as using his professional skills in maintaining the building and grounds, he also leads prayers and services – and cooks the best fry-ups for the regular men's breakfasts!

Jason had always been loyal to his family. As a Christian, he now has a new church family to look out for. Many of the older and more vulnerable members of the congregation – those with mental health struggles or special needs – have found a new friend. Lorna and Jason are always happy to give them lifts, phone them up or help practically. 'They all seem to come to us. It's nice. I never really spoke to anyone like that before. It's a blessing that they trust us and like us. I love to do things for them, look after them and look out for them.' Jason and Lorna took one lady with special needs to see her choice of film at the cinema, even though, as Jason says, 'Peter Rabbit's not really my thing!'

This new life – living for God – should not only be lived in the Christian bubble at church, but all day, every day – at home, at work, with friends and family. For Jason, that was tough. He realised that his old way of running his business was not compatible with following Jesus. Big changes were needed. 'Because I was running a building firm with a lot of rough lads, I found myself still shouting and getting angry with people, and that was in conflict with my faith. I was thinking, "I can't carry on like this." It didn't feel right, the way I was dealing with things. It seemed the only way people would listen was if I was shouting or being threatening towards them. That weren't working for me anymore. So I basically got rid of everybody. I still had about twenty-four blokes working for me when I become a Christian and I cut that down to three.'

This wasn't a decision Jason made rashly; he prayed about it. 'I was praying to God for three to four weeks. My thoughts were to just make the firm smaller and move the office to the end of the garden. I woke up one morning and just knew what to do. It was to change the firm completely and start again. It was quite scary because I didn't have a lot of money round me at the time. I was probably about three years in of being a Christian. We kind of built it from there. Now there is ten of us altogether, which is where I want it. We didn't want people who were argumentative. We just wanted people who would do a day's work, be part of the team and move it forward.'

Things went well until the Covid lockdown. 'In the last lockdown we was going to lose everything. Everything was going to be gone – the house, the business and everything. There was no way out this time. I've been in debt to the tune of half a million and got out of it, but this time I was too small as a business – there was only six of us then. It had gone too far. We give it to the Lord, as we always do as a family. We said, "Lord, this ain't going to change how we feel about you. What happens happens. Give us the strength to get through it. Be with us and help us." We give it to God. I know I'm not the strong one. I know God's character. I know who God is. I can trust him. You can live by his Word. Whatever he says, he doesn't break promises. What he says, he does.' Yet again Jason and his family saw God help them through a difficult time. 'We've come through it and been truly blessed since then. The firm's in a really good place now. I don't know what's going to happen tomorrow or next week. I'm happy with the way things are. Now I don't have to shout and holler anymore.'

As a result of him becoming a Christian, Jason's social life has changed too. During the dark years following his mother's death, his wild nights out had been exchanged for nights in drinking and taking drugs alone. Nonetheless he found it hard when the invitations to join his friends in the pub dried up. 'I know my phone stopped ringing. I used to get ten to twenty calls a day sometimes, particularly when it was coming to the weekend. People would ring me up to go out for a drink and things. That stopped very quickly after becoming a Christian – when I kept saying no. It's hard to deal with at first because you feel kinda lonely. That's a tough one. It took me most of my Christian life so far to get used to that. But I found new things to do. I go fishing now. I'm busy with the church, specially being District Warden. There's a lot of responsibility there.' And Roy – who Jason once dismissed as a 'nice old bloke … talking rubbish', when he went to their house for baptism preparation years before – has become a valued friend and mentor.

Given his past addiction, Jason knows that socialising with old friends would be risky, but he keeps in touch and longs for them to know Jesus for themselves. His past reputation means many of the old crowd are cynical or incredulous about Jason's new life. He knows that it will take a lot to convince them that he really has changed. 'I did have a reputation. I still have. Where I come from, people don't think that people can change. It takes a long time for people to change their mind. Integrity for a Christian is so important, particularly if others are looking at you. If you are going to be a light to them, you have to change. It's a tough walk sometimes. I've had my struggles with it.'

Jason knows he has to live a new life with his family and friends, but he also knows they need to hear the good news of Jesus that is behind his transformation. He takes every opportunity. In the van, on the way to a job with his team, he listens to a Christian radio station to provoke conversation. Roofing work means his men are a captive audience. Some showed early interest, but then backed off as old habits and addictions proved too powerful. Others are intrigued and curious. Some of the least likely have responded more positively – even while Jason was still on drugs and living a less than consistent life. 'Steve was one of the biggest drug dealers in this area. I hadn't seen him for a while. He went away for eight years for drugs. He come out, but he had cancer – a big tumour on his stomach. I started talking to him. I loved him – he was a good mate. I was still taking drugs then – I used to get em off him! – but I was a Christian. I started talking to him about Jesus one day – with a gramme of coke in me. I mean, it don't make sense! But I kept talking to him. In the end I stopped the drugs, and I told him what happened.'

Eventually matters came to a head for Steve. 'He had a fight – he had hit someone with a machete – and someone had kicked his door in. I sent some of the lads out to put in a big fire door because he was worried about them coming through his front door. He was dying at the same time. I used to ring him up and talk to him about Jesus. He said he felt lonely, and it was quite sad really. Then the Sunday night, I got a phone call from his missus saying Steve's in hospital. Me and Lorna went to bed. We had just been talking about Steve. We prayed that Steve would come to know Jesus before he died. Within ten minutes of the prayer the phone rang, and it was Steve. He said, "Send the vicar up here, I want to speak to him." I said I would have a chat with David and see if he would come up. David went up to see him.' In the hospital David explained that no one is too bad to be forgiven by Jesus; that it is never too late to trust in Jesus and be welcomed home by our heavenly Father. Steve prayed with David. It looks like Jason's prayer for his friend was answered just in time. Steve died shortly after and Jason trusts that he is now at peace in heaven with God, his heavenly Father.

Why does Jason keep talking to his friends about Jesus, when so few want to listen? He certainly wants them to know the forgiveness and new life that he has experienced for himself, but his motivation also comes from a darker time in his life. Jason sees the disturbing occult events in his home as a glimpse of hell. But hell – the destination of all who have not trusted in Jesus for forgiveness – will be far worse. In this world God's power, goodness and protection are at work. In hell they are entirely absent. 'I know what's at stake. I've seen demons – real demons. Trust me, you don't want to be in a room alone with them. I have seen demons. I have felt their presence. I have been in their presence. And it's an evil that I've never experienced before. It is terrifying. I had protection from God – that's why they couldn't do what they really wanted to do. But when you die, that protection's gone if you don't know Jesus.'

Still, many people won't listen to Jason's warning. 'That's what pushed me on. People don't understand. I see how evil they think and the things they do. They torment and just think it's fun. In hell you are in a bad, bad place. I get some people saying, "I'll love it in there. I'll have a right laugh." Trust me, they [demons] don't like you. They just want to destroy you. That is what drives me. I was protected and they won't be. That's why I keep telling them. They may think I'm mad – a lot of em do.'

Jason is worried about his friends' eternal destination, but the benefits of trusting Jesus in this life are compelling too. 'If someone said I was to die tomorrow, that would be fine. I would be OK with that. But if someone said you could live all your life again, have all the riches you want and live until you are ninety but you can't follow Jesus, I'd rather have this seven years than any other years in my life. It's life-changing. It's the only time in my life I can truly say, hand on heart, that I've been happy – truly happy. There were times when I had a laugh and things, but I never ever have really been happy in my life' – until now. When Jason gave his life to Jesus, it was Jesus who changed his life. 'People don't just change like that. It's a spiritual thing. It's from the Lord.'

For Jason, happiness is not even the best thing about being a Christian. 'Peace, peace of mind, is the best thing. There is ups and downs, but you'll never get peace like being a Christian. You can drink and take as many drugs as you like – you're not going to find that peace you find once it's all out in the open with Jesus. Not only that you go to heaven when you die! It is just full of hope – just so much hope in giving yourself to the Lord fully.'

Perhaps the difference that Jesus has made in Jason's life can be best seen in his reaction to the recent death of his father. After the death of his brother, Kevin, Jason had wanted revenge – to kill the dealer who had bitten him and caused his death. Jason's anger and guilt meant the wake turned into a battleground. Then when his mother died, Jason was unable to cope with his grief. The depression and drug use that followed led to his attempt to contact her using a Ouija board app, with disastrous consequences.

How would Jason handle his father's death? Jason's father had made his childhood a misery, and Jason had blamed him for causing his mother pain and unhappiness. He had still been Jason's role model, even if a negative one, and he had set the pattern for Jason's life of criminality. Grief is always a complicated emotion. What difference would his faith make this time round?

'It's made a massive difference. You know what happened when my mum died and my brother. With my dad, I spoke to him about Jesus. He said to me that he had said the prayer and got on his knees. That was a few years back. Whether he really did or not I don't know. It's between him and God, not me. When he passed, he was suffering – he was ready to go. Could I have done more? Maybe. I used to pray for him. I've told him about Jesus many times. I've invited him to church. Once he just said, "The seats are too hard." That made me laugh. That was him.'

During his long struggle with cancer and dementia, Jason made sure his father was cared for financially and practically. Then when it came to planning his dad's funeral service, Jason wanted 'God involved'. 'David done a great service. Everyone enjoyed the service. I didn't think they would. It just shows ya. When the Word of God is preached, people can't help but love it. It's our music. The gospel is our music. When you hear it, it's like an old tune. There's something that draws you to it. The gospel is in us all, and you just have to hear it the right way. Told as it is supposed to be told, it's like hearing an old tune again. These are people who don't know Jesus. I come out of there feeling good. I didn't feel hateful or angry or any of them feelings I used to have. I forgave him. I was able to let it all go. We went down the pub after and I had a couple of beers – which I hadn't for a long time – with the lads and some family, which was nice. I woke up in the morning and I felt good.

'I've just lost my dad, but I got a new one a few years ago – a heavenly Father. I loved my dad. He had his faults, but it is what it is. But God and Jesus is a whole lot better. Jesus will make you into a proper man – a real man, with strength, determination. He gives you all them qualities – to love others; to be kind, actually going out and doing things for people. It's easy to be horrible to people. Jesus gives you that opportunity to be a better person.'

Jason has made the most of every opportunity God has given him to be that better person. Here are just a few words from some of Jason's new church family that show the difference God has made to his life – and through him to the lives of others. Margaret, a widow in her eighties with mobility issues, had tears in her eyes as she described Jason: 'So caring and kind, and shows so much love.' Tony, an Oxford-educated lawyer, and Jason's Bible study group leader: 'He's such a testament to God's transforming power and his grace – an inspiration to us in terms of his maturity and compassion and love.' Janet, who has autism and learning difficulties: 'He is supportive and helps people with disabilities. He understands people with autism.'

Dozens of others would have made similar comments. Love, compassion and support are the words frequently used to describe a man who, just a few years earlier, said he didn't know how to love. Previously he 'showed' love by hurting those who he thought threatened his family. Now he shows love by talking to those others often have no time for; by practically helping out people with no family to look after them; and by putting the needs of others before his own.

Jason thought he would be the last on God's list. He never believed that God would be interested in someone like him. He had the impression, like many others, that God is only interested in respectable people. Reading through Luke's Gospel, in the few days after that very first meeting with David, showed him that has never been the case. When God came to earth – when Jesus came as a human baby – the first people to visit were not the respectable citizens of Bethlehem – they turned Mary and Joseph away. The first visitors were unrespectable shepherds, who lived life on the margins. When he grew up, Jesus spent time with prostitutes and traitors, and was hated by the religious establishment. In Luke's Gospel (chapter 19, verse 10) Jesus says he came 'to seek and to save the lost'. Jesus came for people just like Jason. The last person who spoke to Jesus, just before his death, was a criminal on the adjacent cross. We don't know why this criminal had received the death penalty, but crucifixion was reserved for the worst crimes. He cried out to Jesus for help, just like Jason did. Jesus replied, 'Today you will be with me in paradise' (Luke 23:43). This criminal – another man who many would think would be last on God's list – was the first person to have his past wiped clean by Jesus' death in his place. And so he was also the first person to enjoy the perfect future that Jesus came to guarantee for everyone who cries out to him for help. Nobody is at the top or bottom of God's list. God longs to help each one of us – to forgive us our past, and to transform our present and future, so we can live the life we were created for. Why not ask for God's help too? What are you waiting for?

WHAT NOW?

If you have read Jason's story and want to know more about how you can get to know Jesus for yourself, read on.

- You may well feel you need more information about who Jesus is and what he has done. Why not read one of the Gospels? Matthew, Mark, Luke and John are the four accounts in the Bible of the life, death and resurrection of Jesus. Jason started with Luke's Gospel. The whole Bible is available online for free on www.biblegateway.com where you can either read the Bible for yourself or listen to it being read.

- It is helpful to be able to ask questions and think about what it means to follow Jesus. Meetings like Christianity Explored are held in many churches. Their website – www.christianityexplored.org – will help you to find one locally. It also has lots of helpful videos answering questions you might have as well as real-life stories of others, like Jason, who have come to know Jesus for themselves.

- Jason got in touch with a local Christian minister. Check out local church websites, making sure you find one that believes in what the Bible teaches, and get in touch. They should be delighted – if not, try another one!

- If you can, go to a service at a church that believes and teaches the Bible. Jason was nervous, but found a warm welcome. Churches are full of people from all different backgrounds who have been forgiven and are being changed by Jesus. God knows we all need help whatever stage we are at. That is what church is for!

You don't have to do any of the things mentioned above to become a Christian. You can pray now, asking Jesus to help you trust and follow him, just as Jason did. Praying is just talking to Jesus. He knows all about you, so there is nothing to hide and no need to try and impress! Just talk – out loud or in your head – as you would talk to a friend. You could pray using these few simple steps:

A Admit – that you have messed up and that you need Jesus' help. Jason had to admit that he couldn't sort his life out himself and that the way he had lived was not the way God had created him to live.

B Believe – that Jesus, by dying on the cross in your place, can forgive you and give you a new start in life. Jason realised that Jesus could forgive him the very worst things he had done. He can forgive you too.

C Commit – to following Jesus! He will help you, but he has also given us things to help us in our new life with him. If you haven't already done so, check out points 1–4 above. Remember that Jesus is always there for you, so talk to him and ask him for help every day!

Here is a prayer you might like to pray if you are not sure what to say:

Dear Lord Jesus,

I am sorry that I have lived my life my way and not yours. I admit that I have messed up and need your help. I believe that you died for me so I can be forgiven and have a new life with you. Please forgive me for all the things I have done that are not what you want – for ignoring you, hurting others and living my life my way rather than your way. Please help me as I start my new life with you. Help me to change to be the person you want me to be.

Amen.

ABOUT THE AUTHORS

Clare Heath–Whyte is a popular speaker at women's events and a Christian biographer. Clare is married to David and serves alongside him at their church in Morden, South London. Her previous books include *Old Wives Tales* and *First Wives Club*.

Jason Armstrong is a South London builder whose life of violence, drugs and criminality was transformed by Jesus. He now serves as warden at David and Clare's church in Morden, South London.

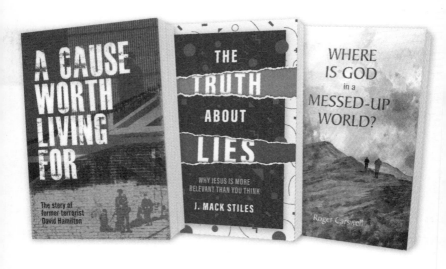